handmade
Glamping

handmade Glamping

Add a touch of glamour to your camping trip
with these 35 gorgeous craft projects

Charlotte Liddle & Lucy Hopping

CICO BOOKS

LONDON NEW YORK

This edition published in 2018 by CICO Books
An imprint of Ryland Peters & Small Ltd

341 E 116th St   20–21 Jockey's Fields,
New York NY 10029   London WC1R 4BW

www.rylandpeters.com

10 9 8 7 6 5 4 3 2

First published in 2013 by CICO Books

Text © Charlotte Liddle and Lucy Hopping 2013
Design and photography © CICO Books 2013

A CIP catalog record for this book is available from
the Library of Congress and the British Library.

ISBN: 978 1 78249 570 3

Printed in China

Editor: Marie Clayton

Design: Louise Turpin

Illustration: Louise Turpin

Technique illustration: Stephen Dew
and Kate Simunek

Photographer: Claire Richardson

Styling: Nel Haynes

Contents

Introduction

For many of us, living in a modern and busy world means juggling a home, career, family, friends, and children. Sometimes this can simply grind us down, forcing us to re-assess how we live our lives and re-organize our priorities. Many of us are looking for an alternative way of life, some are simply looking for a short weekend escape or want their own retreat hidden at the bottom of the backyard. Whether you are a seasoned crafter or just dabbling for the first time, our hope is that this book will provide you with all the inspiration you need to create your own amazing space. We have designed the projects to cover a wide range of traditional crafts but with a modern twist. Techniques such as sewing, embroidery, knitting, crochet, and patchwork are used to create quirky, retro, and "vintage" items that you can make to decorate your motorhome, caravan, cabin, tent, or beach hut.

The book features 35 easy-to-follow step-by-step projects and is split into four chapters. In the first chapter, **Recycling and Repurposing**, we hope to inspire you to look at things around you with new eyes. It is brimming with creative ways to restyle your interior space by showing you how to cover ugly seats, or craft unusual pillows, blinds, tablecloths, and more. We move outside for the second chapter, **Campfire Cooking**, to make a beautiful picnic carrybag, coasters, placemats, and other fun dining accessories. Designed with a 1950s color palette in mind, the projects are bold and quirky.

Chapter three, **Pretty Decorations**, is a frivolous and fun collection of projects—here we show you how to create those finishing touches to really make your space unique. Create dreamcatchers, a fabric clock, colorful bunting, and glass jar storage. To emphasize the playful nature of these items, the colors are zesty and bright with hints of neon. Our inspiration in the final chapter, **Outdoor Living**, was the seaside. Soft muted tones, stripes, and shirting fabrics provide the basis for a range of nautical-themed projects. Ideas include a crochet picnic blanket, an upcycled deckchair, and a stylish appliqué windbreak.

It's not just about the finished article in this book—we want you to enjoy the actual process of making and taking time out for yourself. The notion that camping is old-fashioned, boring, and damp is long-gone. Eco campsites, wooden pod sites, and "Glamping" (Glamorous camping) sites are popping up all over the place to provide comfortable, nostalgic, and quirky vacations in the great outdoors. Over the past couple of years we have seen the "staycation" rapidly become a favorite choice for many who are proud to spend their vacations in their home country. Creating your own oasis and personalizing it to your taste will make it more of a sanctuary for you, your family, and friends. So why not take your stash of materials and this book along on your next "staycation?" You will be no doubt be inspired by your surroundings as well as by these projects, which will help you to create your very own personal *Handmade Glamping* experience.

introduction

CHAPTER 1

Recycling and Repurposing

This section is full of inspiring ideas to help you redecorate your caravan, campervan or motorhome, giving it a whole new lease of life. The projects include a simple blind, seat cover, and recycled vintage curtains, all of which can be adapted to suit your own color scheme. In this chapter you will also find vibrant decorative accessories in a range of different techniques, such as a braided rag rug, a patchwork tablecloth, and a knitted bow pillow cover. Follow the instructions and make yourself a truly glamorous camping retreat that will be the envy of the campsite.

Honeycomb patchwork pillow

Give an old lace tablecloth a new lease of life as a pretty pillow cover. Use coordinating fabrics for the patchwork hexagons.

GATHER TOGETHER

Template on page 136

Stiff paper

7 pieces of patterned fabric, each measuring 16 x 3 in. (40 x 8 cm)

Scissors

Thread and hand sewing needle

5 pieces of Bondaweb, each measuring 8 x 8 in. (20 x 20 cm)

Iron

18 x 18 in. (46 x 46 cm) piece white lace tablecloth fabric

2 pieces of white cotton fabric, each measuring 18 x 18 in. (46 x 46 cm)

16 in. (40 cm) white zipper

Sewing machine

Zipper foot attachment

74 in. (184 cm) deep pink pompom trim

18 small white lace flowers, cut from a length of white flower trim (optional)

18 coordinating sequins and beads (optional)

18 in. (46 cm) pillow form (cushion pad)

WHAT TO DO

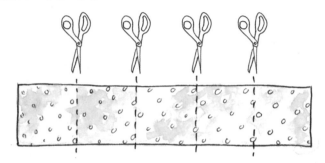

1 Using the template cut 35 hexagons from stiff paper. Cut each of the patterned fabrics into five 3-in. (8-cm) squares to create 35 squares. Pin a paper hexagon to the WS of each fabric square and cut around it, leaving a ½-in. (1-cm) border.

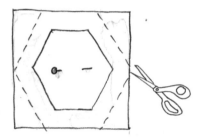

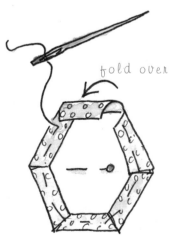

fold over

2 Fold the fabric border over the paper template and baste (tack) the fabric to the paper template, making sure each corner is folded neatly whilst basting. Repeat with another six hexagons and then arrange them into a circular patch.

3 With RS together, overstitch the outer hexagons around the central hexagon in order (only stitch one edge of the hexagon before moving on to the next one.) With RS together stitch the outer hexagons together at the seams. Press the patch and remove all the basting stitches.

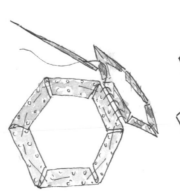

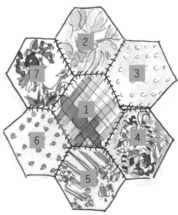

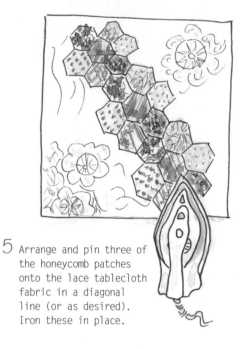

4 Place the patch onto a square of Bondaweb
  and draw around it. Cut the Bondaweb out and
  iron it onto the back of the patch, following
  the manufacturer's instructions. Peel away
  the paper backing. Repeat Steps 2–4 to make
  a total of five honeycomb patches (three
  for the front of the cushion and two to go
  underneath the lace areas).

5 Arrange and pin three of
  the honeycomb patches
  onto the lace tablecloth
  fabric in a diagonal
  line (or as desired).
  Iron these in place.

6 Place one white fabric piece underneath
  the lace tablecloth fabric and arrange the
  two remaining honeycomb patches between
  the two layers so that the color shows
  through the lace areas. Press to secure
  the honeycomb patches in place. Pin and
  baste the lace fabric to the solid white
  fabric around the edge.

recycling and repurposing

7 To insert the zipper into the back of the pillow cover, take the other piece of white fabric and cut in half. Place the two pieces RS together and pin. Using a ⅝ in. (1.5 cm) seam allowance, machine stitch 1½ in. (4 cm) in from each end.

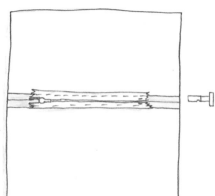

8 Open out and press the seams open. Pin and baste the zipper into the opening and machine stitch in place, using a zipper foot. Open the zipper half way.

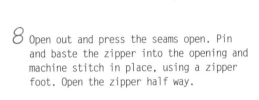

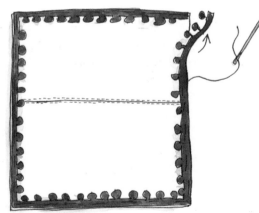

9 Cut the pompom trim into four equal lengths and then pin and baste each length around the edges of the backing piece. Place the back and front pillow cover pieces together with RS together. Pin and machine stitch around all four sides. Neaten seams and remove basting threads.

10 Turn the pillow cover RS out through the open zipper and press. For a pleasing final touch, stitch a lace flower and sequin or bead to each point of the three central hexagons on the front. Insert the pillow pad through the zipper opening.

Vintage tablecloth curtains

A vintage tablecloth makes a gorgeous pair of curtains; adjust the measurements to suit and find unusual buttons for the tabs.

GATHER TOGETHER

48 x 48 in. (120 x 120 cm) vintage embroidered tablecloth

48 x 48 in. (120 x 120 cm) plain white tablecloth

Scissors

Small piece of cardstock

10 pieces of floral fabric, each one at least 6½ x 8 in. (16 x 20 cm)

Sewing machine

20 buttons

Hand-sewing needle

Pink stranded embroidery floss (thread)

2 strips of fabric, 21 x 5 in. (52 x 13 cm)

4 lengths of 1-in. (2.5-cm) wide ribbon, each 4 in. (10 cm) long

WHAT TO DO

1 Press both of the tablecloths. Look carefully at the vintage tablecloth —if there is an embroidered design decide how to place it. Cut both of the tablecloths in half to create two outer curtains and two pieces of lining. Each piece should measure 48 x 24 in. (120 x 60 cm). If you cut pieces from a larger tablecloth you may need to hem along the bottom and both sides by pressing ⅝ in. (1.5 cm) to the WS and machine stitching in place.

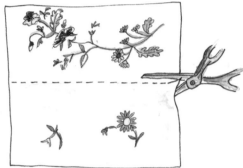

2 Make a template in cardstock measuring 6½ x 3 in. (16 x 8 cm) for the tabs. Fold each piece of patterned fabric in half, place the tab template on top and draw round it. Cut through both layers of fabric to create two identical tabs, one for each curtain. Repeat with the other pieces of fabric to create ten identical pairs of tabs.

3 Fold a tab in half lengthwise with RS together. Pin and machine stitch along the long raw edge, trim seams, and turn RS out. Fold in half to create a tab and press. Repeat with all 20 tabs.

4 Lay the embroidered curtains RS up and pin ten tabs along the top edge of each curtain, facing downward, so all raw edges of the fabric are aligned. Position the first tabs at the edges and make sure the rest are evenly spaced (there should be a gap of about 3½ in./9 cm between each tab).

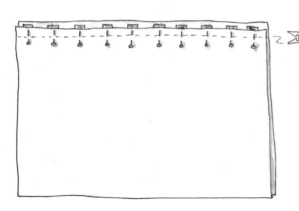

5 Place the lining pieces on top of the curtains RS facing and re-pin the tabs through all layers. Machine stitch along the top edge of each curtain. Press seams and turn RS out.

6 Hand stitch a button onto each tab using the pink embroidery floss (thread).

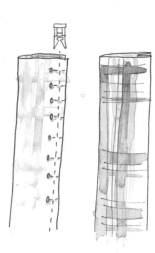

7 Take the two pieces of fabric for the tiebacks and fold each in half lengthwise to make a tube. Pin and machine stitch along the raw edge. Turn RS out and the tuck the raw edges inside the tube. Press.

Make the tiebacks in a fabric that picks up some of the colors in the embroidery. You could use some of the same fabric for one or more tabs.

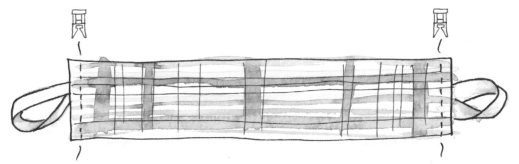

8 Take a length of ribbon and fold into a loop. Insert the ribbon loop in either end of the tieback and machine stitch in place. Repeat with the other ribbons.

vintage tablecloth curtains

Colorful rag rug

Create a colorful rag rug using strips of fabric in a range of bright patterns. Simply braid them together and stitch into shape.

WHAT TO DO

Tear

1 Tear all the fabrics into 1-in. (2.5 cm) wide strips—use scissors to snip into the fabric to begin the tear. Roll the strips into balls to prevent them getting knotted while you work. Do not attach the strips together at this stage, because it is easier to braid them in shorter lengths.

Sew

2 Take three different color strips, stack on top of one another, and stitch them securely together across one end.

Braid

3 Loosely braid the three strips together until you are almost at the end of the first lengths. To attach the next strips, cut a slit in the end of the existing strips and at both ends of the new strips.

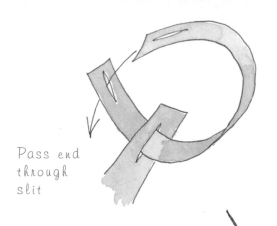

Pass end
through
slit

4 Thread a new strip through the slit in the existing strip and pull the end through the slit in the other end to secure. Repeat with the other two strips and continue braiding. Continue in this way until you have used up all your strips, alternating the colors as you go.

Fold braid over itself
and sew together

5 Fold the first 24 in. (60 cm) of the braid in half so that the sides are touching and hand stitch them together using invisible slipstitch.

Tuck end into the back
of the rug

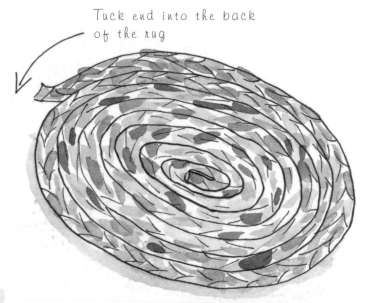

6 Continue stitching the rug together around this initial line of braiding until an oval shape starts to form. Remember to lay the braids side-by-side to keep the rug flat! When you have stitched all the braids together tuck the raw end of the strips into the back of the rug. Press the rug flat.

7 Apply Bondaweb to the piece of felt and iron in place. Lay the rag rug on top of the felt and trace round the edge. Cut the bonded felt to this shape and peel off the paper backing. Apply to the reverse of the rug and iron in place.

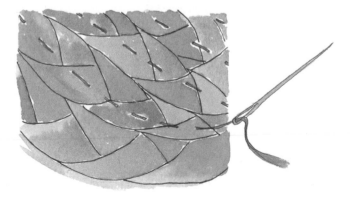

8 Using stranded embroidery floss (thread) and starting from the center, work running stitch along the whole length of the braid to keep the fabric braid and felt backing layer firmly together.

Fabric-covered seating

These seat covers are a cost-effective way to achieve a dramatic change of style, and look stunning made in big bold prints.

GATHER TOGETHER

5½ yd (5 m) piping cord

5½ yd (5 m) white bias binding

Scissors

Sewing machine

Zipper foot attachment

2 rectangles of fabric for the top and bottom, each measuring 35 x 13½ in. (88 x 34 cm)

2 strips of fabric for the back, each measuring 35 x 2⅜ in. (88 x 6 cm)

20 in. (50 cm) zipper

2 strips of fabric for the sides, each measuring 13½ x 4 in. (34 x 10 cm)

1 strip of fabric for the front, measuring 35 x 4 in. (88 x 10 cm)

Foam seat pad

NOTE

These measurements are to cover a seat pad that is 33 x 12½ in. (83 x 31 cm). The material quantities given may need to be adjusted depending on the size of your seat pillow.

WHAT TO DO

1 Cut the piping cord and bias binding into two 2¾ yd (2.5 m) lengths. Open out a length of bias binding, insert the cord into the center and fold the binding around it. Using the zipper foot, machine stitch along the binding, trapping the cord in place. Repeat with the other length of cord and bias binding.

2 With the join at the back of the seat pad, pin and baste (tack) one length of piping cord around the edge of one large piece of fabric on the RS, making sure the cord edge of the piping is facing inward and all the raw edges are aligned. At the join, fold back the bias binding and trim the cord ends so they butt together. Turn under one end of the binding and overlap the raw edge of the other end. Machine stitch the piping in place. Repeat this step to attach the other piping cord to the other large piece of fabric.

3 To insert the zipper into the back panel, place the two narrow strips of fabric RS together. On one long side, machine stitch for 7½ in. (19 cm) in from both ends, leaving the center section unstitched. Open out and press the seam open.

4 Pin and tack the zipper onto the WS of the fabric centered over the open part of the seam. Using a zipper foot attachment, machine stitch around the zipper to secure it in place.

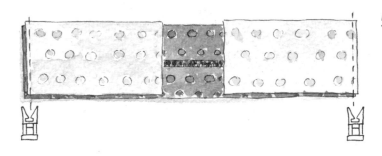

5 With RS together, pin the two shorter side panels onto the ends of the back panel. Machine stitch along the ends to attach the pieces together, then add the long front panel to the ends of the side panels in the same way.

6 Place the rectangle that you have just stitched together onto of the piped pieces with RS together. Pin, baste, and then machine stitch around all edges. Take care to stitch close to the piping cord to ensure a neat finish. Open the zipper fully in preparation for the next step.

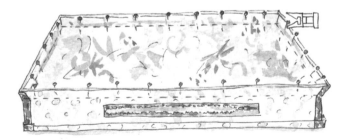

7 Place the other piped piece on top of the rectangle with RS together. Pin and baste around all edges and then machine stitch in place. Trim all seams and turn the seat cover RS out through the zipper opening.

8 Insert the foam seat pad into the cover through the open zipper. Close the zipper and press to get rid of any creases.

Patchwork tablecloth

A patchwork piece like this is very versatile; it can be used as a tablecloth or packed in your bag and used as a picnic blanket.

recycling and repurposing

GATHER TOGETHER

24 x 24 in. (60 x 60 cm) of each of 9 different fabrics

Scissors

Sewing machine

24 in. (60 cm) square Vilene stitch-and-tear

Template on page 137

White machine embroidery floss (thread)

Free-motion embroidery foot

9 coordinating buttons

Sewing needle and thread

Pink, blue, and green (or coordinating) embroidery floss (thread)

8 yd (7.2 m) crochet/lace trimming

2 yd (1.8 m) square piece of vintage bed sheet

WHAT TO DO

1 Cut each of the fabrics into nine 8 in. (20 cm) squares. Arrange the first row of nine patches as desired, mixing fabrics for a pleasing effect. Place the first and second squares RS together and stitch along the right-hand edge. Keep adding squares to the right-hand edge to create the first strip of patchwork. Press out seams.

Just one thing...

If you have a rotary cutter you will be able to cut several layers of fabric at once, which makes cutting the squares much faster and more accurate.

There is generally no need to pin or baste squares together before stitching, but make sure seams are aligned where they intersect.

2 Use the pattern of the first strip as a guide for all the remaining strips. I have made the pattern so that the patches run in a diagonal pattern but you can arrange them as desired. Follow Step 1 to create all nine strips. Place the first and second strips together, RS facing, and machine stitch along the bottom edge. Fold out and press the seam open. Add the other strips in the same way until you have a piece of patchwork that is nine squares by nine squares.

3 Cut nine squares of Vilene stitch-and-tear slightly smaller than the patchwork squares. Trace the daisy template onto each of the squares of stitch-and-tear and pin onto the back of one fabric square per strip.

4 Set up the sewing machine with embroidery floss wound onto the bobbin and normal sewing thread on top. Swap the straight stitch foot for a free-motion embroidery foot attachment. Stitch over the daisy pattern drawn onto the Vilene—this technique is called reverse embroidery and will create a couched outline effect on the RS of the fabric. Repeat for all nine flowers.

Just one thing...

Use flat buttons at the center of the daisy, or use a large sequin instead.

Avoid poor quality embroidery floss for the stitching because the color may bleed when the tablecloth is washed.

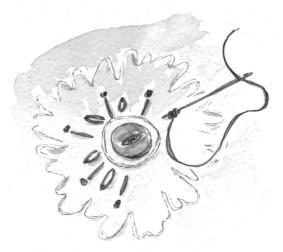

5 Stitch a button into the center of each daisy and add some hand embroidery stitches as extra embellishment. I have used simple straight stitches and French knots.

lay backing on top

6 Cut the crochet/lace trimming into four equal strips and lay onto the edges of the patchwork as shown, with the decorative edge of the trim facing into the center. Place the piece of vintage backing fabric onto the patchwork, RS together, and machine stitch around all edges, making sure you leave a gap (the length of one patch) open for turning.

7 Turn the patchwork RS out and press in place. Slipstitch the gap closed.

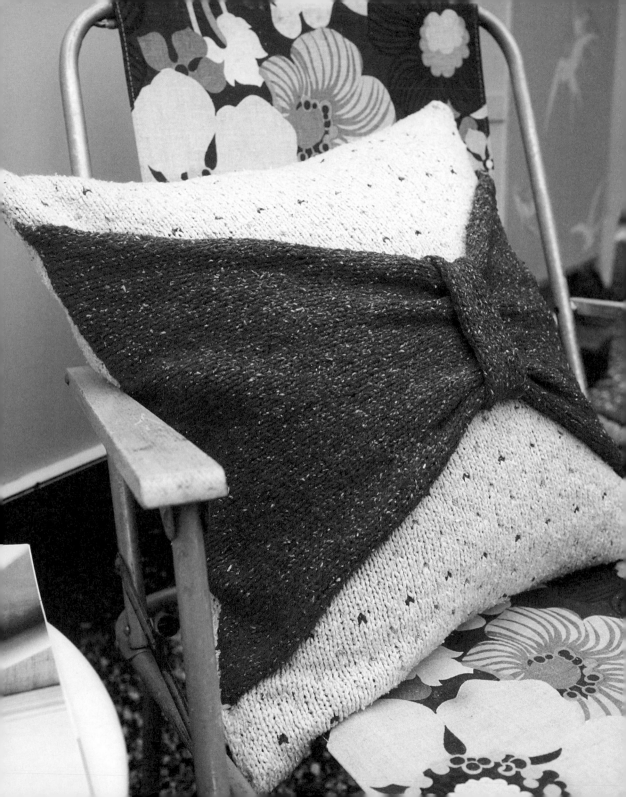

Knitted pillow

Spruce up those canvas camping chairs with this bright
knitted pillow decorated with a cute bow!

WHAT TO DO

1 For the base cover, cast on 84 stitches in cream. **Row 1:**
Purl. **Row 2:** Attach turquoise yarn. Knit 3 stitches in cream,
then *1 stitch in turquoise, 5 stitches in cream; rep from
* all along the row. Tie and break off turquoise yarn. **Rows
3-5:** Work stockinette (stocking) stitch. Attach the pink
yarn. **Row 6:** Knit 6 stitches in cream, then *1 stitch in
pink, 5 stitches in cream; rep from * all along the row.
Tie and break off the pink yarn. **Rows 7-9:** Work stockinette
(stocking) stitch. Repeat Rows 2-9 using lime green and lilac
yarns. Continue repeating Rows 2-9 in alternate color sets
until knitting measures 40 in. (1 m) in length, or wraps
around the pillow pad with an overlap. Finish with a row of
purl. Change to turquoise. **Next row:** *Knit 3, purl 3; rep
from * along the row. Repeat this row another nine times.
Bind (cast) off.

2 For the bow piece, cast on 60 stitches in pink and work
stockinette (stocking) stitch for 20 rows. **Row 21:** *Knit
4, knit 2 together* along the whole row. (50 stitches)
Work stockinette (stocking) stitch for 20 rows. **Row
42:** *Purl 3, knit 2 together* along the whole row. (40
stitches) Work stockinette (stocking) stitch for 40 rows.
Row 83: *Knit 3, increase once* along the whole row. (50
stitches) Work stockinette (stocking) stitch for 20 rows.
Row 104: *Knit 4, increase one stitch; rep from * along
the whole row. (60 stitches) Work stockinette (stocking)
stitch for 20 rows. Cast off.

3 For the center tie ring, cast on 10 stitches in pink
and work stockinette (stocking) stitch until the piece
measures approximately 6 in. (15 cm). Bind (cast) off.
Fold in half and stitch the short ends together to create
a ring of knitting.

Slide tie ring
into center

4 To assemble the pillow,
thread the center tie
ring onto the bow piece
and push to the middle
to make a bow shape.

5 Wrap the base cover around
the pillow pad so that the
ribbing runs across the
center back of the pillow.

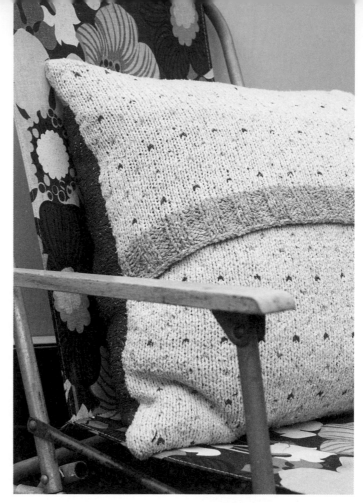

6 Turn the pillow over and
pin the bow to the side
edges, making sure that it
falls at the center front
of the cushion. Stitch in
position with pink yarn,
being careful not to stitch
into the pillow pad.

7 Take the knitting off
the pillow pad and turn
it inside out, ensuring
that the ribbing is in
the inside, and then pin
together. Stitch along the
sides only using cream yarn.
Turn RS out and insert the
pillow pad through the back
overlap opening.

Just one thing...

When sewing on the
bow and stitching the
cover together, do
not pull the yarn too
tightly as you work
or the seams will be
very stiff. Ideally they
should stretch with the
knitting itself.

Yarn and felt flower wreath

A brightly colored fun floral wreath is a wonderful way to welcome guests to your caravan.

GATHER TOGETHER

10 in. (25 cm) diameter polystyrene ring (with flat back)

Pen

1 oz (25 g) hank of yarn in each of pink, green, and blue

Tape

Scissors

Templates on page 136

Felt sheets in each of cream, bright pink, blue, pale pink, light green, olive green, gray

Floral fabric scraps

Assorted sequins

Needle and sewing thread

Small button from fabric-cover button kit

Green stranded embroidery floss (thread)

12 in. (30 cm) ribbon

Thumb tack (drawing pin)

WHAT TO DO

1 Using a pen, mark the sequence of different color yarns on the wreath. Tape the first color to the back and start wrapping—the flowers will be stitched onto the yarn, so wrap two or three times to get a good background. Fix the end of the second color under the last few wraps of the first, then fasten off the first color end with a piece of tape, covering this as you continue wrapping. Repeat until the wreath is completely covered.

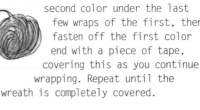

2 For Flower 1, use template A to cut one flower from cream and one from bright pink felt. Use template B to cut one flower from a scrap of floral fabric. Layer the flowers. Cut a small circle of blue felt and place in the center of the top flower, add a sequin and stitch through it to secure.

3 For Flower 2, use template C to cut a rectangle from pale pink felt. Fold in half lengthwise and work running stitch along one edge. Make small cuts ¼ in. (5 mm) apart along the opposite edge, almost to the line of stitching.

4 Roll up the fringed felt strip to form a flower shape and secure with a few stitches through the base.

Just one thing...

Choose yarn and fabric colors to coordinate with your own color scheme, or make different wreaths for different seasons. White, silver and gold would look stunning for a Christmas wreath, and a selection of rich autumnal colors would also work very well.

Use colorfast fabrics and felt and your wreath should survive most weather conditions when hung outside.

5 For Flower 3, use template B to cut one flower from light green felt and one from floral fabric. Cover the button with bright pink felt following the instructions in the kit. Layer up the felt and fabric flowers and stitch together with the button in the center to secure.

6 For Flower 4, use template E to cut one flower from pale green, one from blue, and one from pale pink felt. Stitch small sequins onto the petals of the pink flower. Use template A to cut one flower from a floral fabric and place on top of the felt flowers. Repeat step 3 to make another fringe flower using bright pink felt. Place on top of the other layers and stitch everything in place.

7 Use template D to cut two leaves from olive green felt. Make running stitch lines for veins using green embroidery floss. For Flower 5, repeat the instructions in step 3 using cream felt.

8 For Flower 6, use template F to cut one flower from gray felt and one from floral fabric, and layer together. Cut a small circle of olive felt and place in the center of the flower, add a sequin and stitch through the center to secure.

9 Stitch the flowers onto the yarn-covered wreath using the photograph on page 33 as a guide. Fold the length of ribbon in half. Attach the folded end of the ribbon to the back of the wreath using a thumb tack.

Roll-down blind

A simple and stylish window covering that is fast to make, with beautiful trims to coordinate with your color scheme.

GATHER TOGETHER

24 in. (60 cm) narrow gingham ribbon

24 in. (60 cm) white trim

28 x 24 in. (70 x 60 cm) floral fabric for blind, or to fit your window

Sewing machine

24 in. (60 cm) mini pompom trim

28 x 24 in. (70 x 60 cm) lining fabric or to fit your blind

4 strips of coordinating fabric

1⅛ yd (1 m) green bias binding

21 buttons

Coordinating embroidery floss (thread)

22½ in. (57 cm) dowel

24 in. (60 cm) adhesive Velcro

24 in. (60 cm) strip of wood

WHAT TO DO

1 Thread the gingham ribbon through the white trim and pin onto the floral fabric approximately 3¼ in. (8 cm) up from the bottom edge. Machine stitch along the top and bottom edges of the trim to attach it to the fabric. Pin the mini pompom trim along the bottom edge of the white trim and machine stitch onto the blind fabric.

Pin pompoms on top

Thread ribbon through lace

2 Place front blind and lining with RS together and machine stitch around all edges, leaving a gap along the top edge for turning. Trim seams, turn RS out and press. Top stitch the gap closed.

3 To make the ties take a strip of coordinating fabric, fold it in half lengthwise with RS together, and press. Machine stitch along the long edge and then turn RS out. Fold the top and bottom edges in, press and top stitch to close. Make another three ties in the same way.

recycling and repurposing

4 Fold the top and bottom edges of the blind over by approximately 3¼ in. (8 cm) and press. Pin two of the ties onto the front top edge of the blind 2¾ in. (7 cm) in from each side. Pin the remaining two ties on the reverse of the blind (directly under the top ties and under the folded edge). Machine stitch along the top edge to hold all the ties in place.

5 For the folded decorative trim make regular pleats 2 in. (5 cm) wide and with a 1¼ in. (3 cm) gap between each pleat along the long strip of bias binding. Pin in place on the blind.

7 Machine stitch the bottom hem and insert the dowel. Apply one half of the adhesive Velcro along the top edge of the blind and the other half onto the strip of wood. The wood can then be attached to the top of the window and the blind can easily be removed for cleaning.

6 Fold the top and bottom edge of each pleat toward the center and machine zigzag stitch down the middle to hold the pleat in place. Using embroidery floss, hand stitch three buttons over the top of each line of zigzag stitching.

8 To close up the blind, tie the matching tie ends under the dowel to hold it at the desired level.

This blind is lined with ordinary plain lining material so although it will screen the window it will not block out daylight completely. If you want to screen incoming light more effectively, consider using blackout lining.

The ties do not need to extend to the bottom of the blind because when it is completely down they can hang free.

Clay heart bunting

Use different materials to imprint a design on this great alternative to traditional fabric, or personalize with letter stamps.

GATHER TOGETHER

Rolling pin

Pack of white oven-bake or air-drying clay

2 large baking sheets

Lace or crochet trimming for imprinting design

Templates on page 136

Knife

Knitting needle

Heart cookie cutter

X letter stamp

Paint or dye in lemon, pink, orange, and turquoise

Selection of paintbrushes

Pearlescent white paint

Craft varnish

2¼ yd (2 m) garden twine

Bodkin needle

Selection of ribbons in lemon, pink, orange, and turquoise

WHAT TO DO

1 Roll out half the clay onto a clean baking sheet, to a thickness of ¼ in. (5 mm). Place the pieces of lace and crochet trimming onto the clay and use the rolling pin to imprint the lace pattern into the clay.

2 Copy the triangle template onto the clay and cut around it with a sharp knife, making sure you go right through the clay. Use the knitting needle to pierce six holes along the top edge of the triangle. Repeat this step to make seven more triangles.

3 On the second baking sheet repeat Step 1 with the remaining clay, but use the cookie cutter to cut nine hearts. Use a knife to trim away any excess clay. Alternatively, use the heart template on page 136. Pierce a single hole in the top center of each heart.

4 Roll out the excess clay and stamp a letter X nine times. Cut out a square around each one and place one into the center of each heart.

5 Bake all the clay shapes following the manufacturer's instructions. If using air-drying clay, leave the shapes to harden according to the manufacturer's instructions.

6 Color the hardened shapes with paint—for delicate shades water it down and apply thin coats. Leave to dry and then lightly brush with white pearlescent paint to highlight the lace/crochet design. When dry, finish with a layer of craft varnish.

7 Use a bodkin needle to thread each of the shapes onto the garden twine, alternating triangles and hearts. Tie the coordinating ribbon into bows on the shapes.

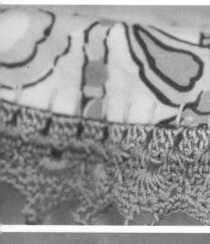

CHAPTER 2

Campfire Cooking

Seasoned campers truly embrace the pleasure of cooking good wholesome food, inside or out. So whether you enjoy toasting bread over a campfire, flipping burgers on a BBQ, or making pots of stew on the camping stove, this chapter will teach you how to make all the kitchen essentials (some may not be so essential but will look lovely!) to help you enjoy those tasty meals with all the family. Try making the picnic bag, recycled fabric basket, or explore some of the crochet and knitting projects to make a vibrant coaster or a kitsch tea cozy.

Striped knitted tea cozy

Knit a vintage-style striped tea cozy to keep your tea hot even on the coldest of days!

GATHER TOGETHER

1 oz (25 g) hank of yarn in each of green, red, yellow, pink, and turquoise

US 6 (4 mm) knitting needles

Pompom template on page 137

Thin card

Scissors

WHAT TO DO

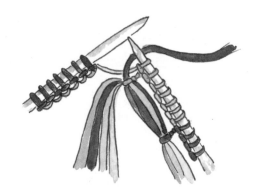

1 Wind each hank of yarn into small ¼-oz (10-g) balls—this will make it much easier to tie the colors together without getting into a mess of tangled yarn and knots. Cast on 120 stitches in Yarn A. Attach the other 4 colors into the knitting by tying them to Yarn A.
Row 1: Knit 12 stitches using Yarn A (the other lengths of yarn should lie at the back of the knitting), then wrap Yarn A around the spare yarns and tie in a loose knot.

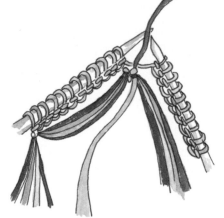

2 Tie Yarn A to Yarn B and knit 12 stitches. Continue with this pattern along the row, tying Yarn B to Yarn C, Yarn C to Yarn D, Yarn D to Yarn E and so on.

3 Start with Yarn E. **Row 2:** Knit 12 stitches then tie a loose knot around the spare yarns as before, but no need to tie Yarn E and D together this time. Bring Yarn E to the WS, take Yarn D to the RS and knit 12 stitches. Continue along the row using Yarn C, B, and A in order.

4 Continue these 2 rows until you have a piece of knitting as long as your teapot is high. For most teapots this is approximately 6 in. (15 cm). By laying the extra yarns along the back of the tea cozy in ⅞ in. (2 cm) lengths, ruffles are created that make a really thick layer to keep your tea warm!

5 Shape the top of the cozy. **Next row:** *Knit 2 together, knit 8, knit 2 together; repeat from * along the row. Remember to wrap the yarn around the bundle of spare yarns as you change color to keep the tea cozy together. (100 sts)

6 **Next row:** *Knit 2 together, knit 6, knit 2 together; repeat from * along the whole row. (80 sts) **Next row:** *Knit 2 together, knit 4, knit 2 together* along the whole row. (60 sts) **Next row:** *Knit 2 together along the whole row. (30 sts) Cut the yarn, leaving an 8-in. (20-cm) length of yarn, thread this through all the remaining stitches on the needle and pull tight to secure. Thread through the stitches a second time and fasten off.

7 Make another piece in the same way. Place the two pieces RS together and sew together along the outside seams, leaving a suitable hole on either side for the spout and handle of the teapot.

8 Use the pompom template on page 137 to make two card rings. Place together and wrap all five yarns alternately through the center hole until it is almost full. Cut the yarn around the edge, slide a 12-in. (30-cm) length of yarn between the two rings, pull tight and tie a double knot. Remove the card and trim any long or loose threads. Sew the pompom to the top of tea cozy.

Crochet food cover

Keep those pesky insects from your tasty delights with this vintage-style crochet food cover.

WHAT TO DO

1 Cut two 9 in. (23 cm) diameter circles from the fabric. Place RS together and sew round the edges using a sewing machine, leaving a gap in the seam of approximately 2 in. (5 cm). Turn RS out and oversew the gap closed by hand. Press flat.

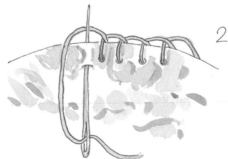

2 Using mustard crochet yarn, work blanket stitch all around the edge of the circle. Each stitch should be evenly spaced, around ¼ in. (5 mm) apart.

NOTE
US and UK crochet patterns share stitch names but these do not refer to the same stitches. This crochet pattern is written using US crochet terminology. See pages 133–135 for details of how to work each stitch.
Single crochet (US) = double crochet (UK)
Double crochet (US) = treble crochet (UK)

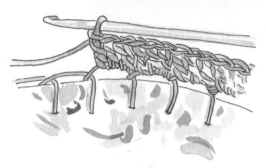

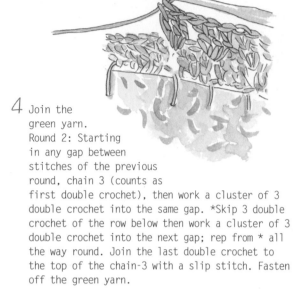

3 Use the mustard yarn and crochet hook. Round 1: Chain 3 (counts as first double crochet), then work 3 double crochet into each blanket stitch. Join the last double crochet to the top of the first chain-3 using a slip stitch. Fasten off the mustard yarn.

4 Join the green yarn. Round 2: Starting in any gap between stitches of the previous round, chain 3 (counts as first double crochet), then work a cluster of 3 double crochet into the same gap. *Skip 3 double crochet of the row below then work a cluster of 3 double crochet into the next gap; rep from * all the way round. Join the last double crochet to the top of the chain-3 with a slip stitch. Fasten off the green yarn.

5 Join in the turquoise yarn. Round 3: Starting in a gap between groups of double crochet in the previous round, chain 3 (counts as first double crochet) and *work 6 double crochet into the first gap of the row below and a single crochet into the next gap; rep from * all the way around. Join the last single crochet to the top of the first chain-3 with a slip stitch.

Just one thing...

When choosing your beads, make sure the hole is big enough to accommodate the yarn easily. Glass beads will add more weight to the edge of the cover, which will help it stay in place better, but plastic beads are perfectly acceptable.

Thread all the beads you will need onto the turquoise yarn, in the correct order, before you begin working the beaded edging and then just pull up the three you need each time you work a beaded stitch.

6 Thread the beads on to the turquoise yarn, starting with one small green bead, then one large blue bead, then one small green bead, repeating this sequence of three beads until all the beads have been threaded on.

7 Turn the work over. Round 4: Starting in a single crochet in the row below, chain 1 (counts as first single crochet) and then *work 4 single crochet into the tops of the stitches below, chain 3.

8 Pull up 3 beads and trap into place using a slip stitch. Chain 3 and single crochet into the fourth double crochet of the scallop, single crochet into the last 2 stitches; rep from * in step 7 all the way round. Join the last single crochet to the first chain-1 with a slip stitch. Fasten off. Sew in all the ends and trim. Iron flat and your cover is complete!

Caravan placemat

This placemat features a little pocket detail to hold your cutlery so you can roll it up to store safely away when not in use.

GATHER TOGETHER

Template on page 138

Pencil

Scissors

10 in. (25 cm) square of Bondaweb

Scraps of coordinating fabric for caravan

Iron

2 pieces of coral cotton fabric, each 17¼ x 12 in. (43 x 30 cm)

6 x 9½ in. (15 x 24 cm) floral fabric for pocket

Sewing machine

Matching sewing thread

17¼ x 12 in. (43 x 30 cm) curtain interlining

Selection of buttons

Needle and stranded embroidery floss (thread)

17¼ in. (43 cm) yellow trim

17¼ in. (43 cm) green trim

40 in. (1 m) coral ribbon

WHAT TO DO

1 Transfer the main outlines of the caravan template onto the Bondaweb backing. Cut the Bondaweb into the three main parts of the caravan body. Trace the door, wheel, and windows onto Bondaweb and cut out.

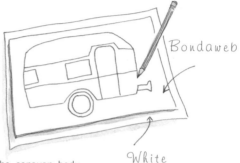

Bondaweb

White paper

2 Iron the Bondaweb pieces to the WS of the fabric scraps following the manufacturer's instructions. Cut around the shapes and layer to create the caravan design on the RS of one piece of coral fabric, positioning it on the right-hand side. Iron in place.

3 Press ¼ in. (5 mm) to the WS along three edges of the pocket fabric and stitch a small double hem along the top. Pin the pocket to the left of the caravan appliqué, then machine stitch down both sides and along the bottom. Machine stitch two vertical lines to create three separate pockets for knife, fork, and spoon.

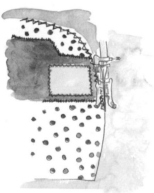

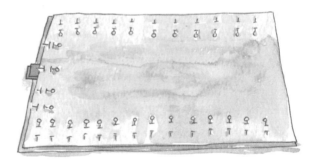

4 Place the curtain interlining under the appliquéd piece and edge the outlines of the appliqué with a closely spaced zigzag stitch. This will pad the placemat slightly and give it a quilted look. Add hand embroidery and buttons as desired.

5 Pin and stitch the trims along the top and bottom of the mat. Cut the ribbon in two and pin with ends aligned to the center left-hand edge. Place the other piece of coral cotton fabric RS down on top of appliquéd piece. Pin and then stitch around the edge, leaving a gap at the bottom for turning. Snip the corners and turn right way out. Slip stitch the gap closed and press.

Crochet coasters

Stylish striped coasters, made using a simple but effective popcorn stitch. The perfect place for your mid-morning coffee cup!

GATHER TOGETHER

Oddments of yarn in red, green, blue, mustard

US E/4 (3.5 mm) crochet hook

Felt

WHAT TO DO

1 Using red yarn, make 4 chain, join with a slip stitch in the first stitch to make a circle. **Round 1:** Chain 1 and then work 12 single crochet into the circle. Join the last stitch to the first stitch using a slip stitch. Change to green yarn. **Round 2:** Chain 4.

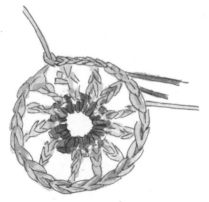

2 Work double crochet in the next stitch and chain 1; repeat this sequence 10 times until you are back to the start and then join to the top of the first stitch with a slip stitch.

NOTE
US and UK crochet patterns share stitch names but these do not refer to the same stitches. This crochet pattern is written using US crochet terminology. See pages 133–135 for details of how to work each stitch.
Single crochet (US) = double crochet (UK)
Double crochet (US) = treble crochet (UK)

3 Change to the blue yarn. **Round 3:** Chain 3. Work 3 double crochet in the same gap, remove the hook from the stitch, insert the hook front to back into the top of the first stitch, then re-hook the end stitch and pull it through to create a popcorn stitch.

4 Chain 2, then work 4 double crochet in the next gap, repeat dropping the stitch, inserting the hook into the front of the stitch and pulling through to create your second popcorn stitch. Repeat this last sequence until you are back to the start and then join to the top of the first popcorn using a slip stitch.

Just one thing...

The popcorn stitch used for these coasters creates a thicker fabric, which means the coasters are well insulated and can be used for hot drinks as well as cold.
   For matching table mats just continue working more rounds until you have the size of circle you need—but remember you will need much more yarn.

5 Change to mustard yarn. **Round 4:** Work 2 popcorn stitches in the first gap, then 1 popcorn in the next gap. Repeat this sequence of 2 and 1 until you get back to the start and then join to the top of the first popcorn using a slip stitch.

6 Change to red yarn. **Round 5:** Work 2 popcorn stitches in the first gap, then 1 popcorn stitch in each of the next 2 gaps. Repeat this sequence of 2, 1, and 1 until you get back to the start and then join to the top of the first popcorn using a slip stitch.

7 Change to green yarn. **Round 6:** Work 2 popcorn stitches in the first gap, then 1 popcorn in each of the next 3 gaps. Repeat this sequence of 2, 1, 1, and 1 until you get back to the start and then join to the top of the first popcorn using a slip stitch. Change to blue yarn. **Round 7:** Work 2 popcorn stitches in the first gap, then 1 popcorn in each of the next 4 gaps. Repeat this sequence of 2, 1, 1, 1, and 1 until you get back to the start and then join to the top of the first popcorn using a slip stitch. Fasten off the yarn by pulling it through the last stitch to secure.

8 Complete your coaster by sewing in the ends and ironing it on the reverse. Cut a round piece of felt to the same size and hand stitch this to the reverse of the coaster. Repeat for another three coasters but change the order of the colors so they all look different!

Fabric basket

This beautiful basket is perfect for storing kitchen essentials such as tea bags, or could be made bigger to use as a fruit basket.

GATHER TOGETHER

Selection of coordinating fabrics

Scissors

6½ yd (6 m) cotton washing line or thick piping cord

Matching sewing thread

Sewing machine

Strong machine needle (for jeans)

4-in. (10-cm) square of green felt

Leaf template page 137

4-in. (10-cm) square of coordinating fabric

4-in. (10-cm) square of Bondaweb

Iron

Selection of beads and sequins

Hand sewing needle

Hot glue gun

WHAT TO DO

1 Cut your fabrics into 20 strips, each one approximately ⅝ x 16 in. (1.5 x 40 cm).

2 Start to wrap the fabric over the end of the washing line. Make sure the end of the cord is securely encased in the fabric and then continue to wrap along the cord tightly.

Wrap

fabric basket

55

3 Set your sewing machine to the widest and longest zigzag stitch. Fold the end of the washing line in and zigzag stitch across the top to hold in place. Continue to wrap and stitch the washing line as you coil it, adding new strips of fabric as necessary.

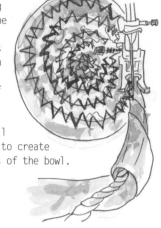

4 Carry on coiling and stitching the base of the bowl until it reaches 4 in. (10 cm) in diameter. Then lift the edge of the base upward and continue to stitch—this will naturally start to create the curved sides of the bowl.

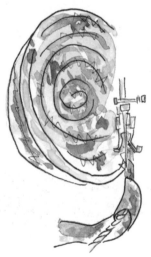

5 Continue to hold the edge of the bowl upward as you sew, wrapping a selection of different colored fabrics onto the bowl as you sew. Work until you reach the end of the washing line. Fold the fabric over and twist to ensure that the end of the washing line is completely encased. Oversew a number of times to secure.

6 Make a 2 in. (5 cm) diameter version of the bowl as a flower embellishment. To make fabric leaves, use the template on page 137 to cut two leaves from green felt and two from patterned fabric. Apply Bondaweb to the felt leaves, peel away the backing paper, and position the fabric leaves on top. Following the manufacturer's instructions, press to bond the two layers together.

7 Fold the bottom of each leaf over so that the point is in the center and then fold lengthwise to create a 3-D leaf shape. Slipstitch along the bottom fold to hold in place. Add beads and sequins, then stitch the leaves onto the main bowl. Use a hot glue gun to attach the flower to the bowl.

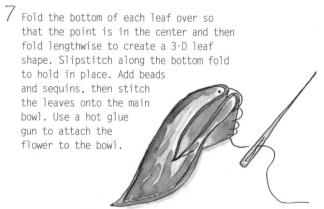

Embroidered dishtowel

Show off your embroidery skills on this beautiful dishtowel.
Almost too pretty to use!

Paper and pen

Template on page 137

Plain cotton dishtowel

Tape

Washable fabric marker pen

Embroidery hoop

Stranded embroidery floss
    (thread) in pink, red,
    purple, orange, yellow,
    lime green, and turquoise

Sewing/embroidery needle

Crochet trim

Rick rack trim

Sewing thread

Iron

WHAT TO DO

1 Trace the embroidery
   template onto a piece
   of paper. Stick this to
   a window and tape your
   dishtowel over it so
   the light coming through
   the window reveals the
   design on the fabric.
   Trace the design onto
   the dishtowel using the
   fabric marker pen.

2 The template suggests a variety of
   embroidery stitches, such as couching, back
   stitch, chain stitch, French knots, satin
   stitch, cross stitch, lazy daisy stitch,
   and leviathan stitch (see pages 129-130).
   Use the photograph opposite as a guide for
   color placement.

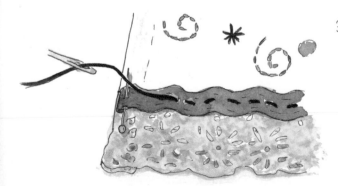

3 Once the embroidery is complete,
   wash off any fabric marker lines
   that still show. Pin the crochet
   trim and rick rack trim along the
   bottom edge of the dishtowel,
   making sure the raw ends are turned
   under at each side. Hand stitch in
   place, using small neat stitches.
   Press flat.

Picnic basket lining

Transform a tired old picnic basket with kitsch print fabrics and cute hanging strawberries. You will be a true glamper!

WHAT TO DO

Fold twice

1 Cut the larger piece of gingham fabric into two 17 x 4 in. (42 x 10 cm) strips and two 13 x 4 in. (32 x 10 cm) strips. Fold one long edge of each strip over twice to make a double hem and stitch in place (these will become the outer edging of the basket).

2 Cut the strawberry fabric into two 17 x 6¾ in. (42 x 17 cm) strips. With RS together, pin a strawberry fabric strip to a matching red gingham strip. Cut the striped fabric into two 13 x 6¾ in. (32 x 17 cm) strips and pin to the shorter gingham strips, RS together. Machine stitch the seams, press and turn out.

Back

Side

Side

Front

3 Pin all the side panels onto the red gingham base fabric with RS facing. Machine stitch the seams, press and turn out.

4 Pin and machine stitch up the four corner seams of the lining. To give the gingham outer edging room to overhang the basket, taper the seam outward slightly at the top as shown.

5 Place the lining into the basket. Mark and cut incisions about 2 in. (5 cm) at the front of the basket for the loops of the basket. Mark and cut slits up the outer gingham edging at the back of the basket to allow for hinges.

Front

Back

6 Measure the incisions made in Step 5 and cut strips of bias binding slightly longer. Press the binding in half. Pin a binding piece to enclose each raw edge and machine stitch in place.

7 Lace the green velvet ribbon through the white cotton trimming and cut off the excess. Fold over the ends of the trimming, press, and pin onto the outer gingham overhang near the lip of the basket. Machine stitch in place.

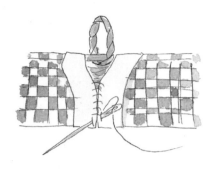

8 Place the lining into the picnic basket and hand stitch the slits below the back hinges.

9 Cut two strawberry shapes in red felt. Embellish with beads, sequins and French knots to represent seeds. Place RS together and machine stitch, leaving the top edge open. Turn RS out.

Pull thread tight

10 Work running stitch around the top edge of the strawberry. Stuff with fiberfill and gather the running stitch to close the top. Knot the ends of the thread together to secure.

11 Cut 8 in. (20 cm) of green velvet ribbon and loop into a star shape, stitching at the center point. Stitch to the top of the strawberry as leaf and stalk.

12 Cut another 8 in. (20 cm) of green velvet ribbon and hand stitch onto the strawberry. Finish with a gingham bow. Repeat Steps 9-12, using the pink felt, to make the other strawberry and tie both together onto the basket.

Picnic carry bag

A huge bag is a necessity for any camping trip; it's perfect for a picnic or to carry the family's swimming kit.

GATHER TOGETHER

2 strips of check fabric each measuring 27 x 7¼ in. (68 x 18 cm)

2 pieces of patterned fabric each measuring 27 x 24 in. (68 x 60 cm)

Sewing machine

2 pieces of blackout lining fabric measuring 27 x 30½ in. (68 x 76 cm)

2 strips of gingham fabric each measuring 36 x 4¾ in. (90 x 12 cm)

2 strips of blackout lining fabric measuring 36 x 4¾ in. (90 x 12 cm)

5 squares of check fabric each measuring 7¼ x 7¼ in. (18 x 18 cm)

5 squares of orange silk fabric each measuring 6¼ x 6¼ in. (16 x 16 cm)

1 side strip of an 18 in. (45 cm) zipper

Hot glue gun

Coordinating button (optional)

WHAT TO DO

1 To make the front of the bag place one strip of check fabric, RS together, onto one of the pieces of patterned fabric, and machine stitch together. Open out and press. Repeat with the other two pieces to make the back of the bag.

2 Place the front and back bag pieces together with RS together. Place a piece of lining fabric underneath and another one on top. Pin in place and then machine stitch round the sides and bottom edges. Trim seams back to neaten.

Just one thing...

The blackout fabric used for the lining is quite heavy duty so it makes the picnic bag stronger than it would be if you used ordinary lining fabric—although a plain lining fabric is quite acceptable if you prefer it. You could also use a plasticized fabric for the lining instead to make your picnic bag waterproof, but do not use it to line the handles because it will not be strong enough.

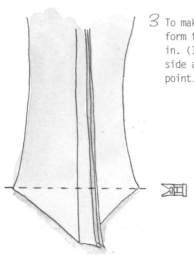

3 To make the gusset, flatten both bottom corners to form two triangles and pin in place. Measure in 4 in. (10 cm) from the point of the corner on each side and machine stitch across the corner at this point. Trim seams and turn the bag RS out.

4 Fold under ¼ in. (1 cm) of the top check fabric band to the inside of the bag all round and press. Fold the check fabric over again to make a double hem and top stitch all the way round the top of the bag to neaten.

5 To make the straps place a strip of gingham fabric and lining fabric RS together and fold in half lengthwise with the gingham on the inside. Machine stitch down the long edge, trim seams and turn RS out. Fold the top and bottom edges under, pin, and press in place. Repeat to make the second strap.

6 To attach the straps to the bag, pin onto the front and back approximately 4¾ in. (12 cm) in from each side. Machine stitch in a box shape, as shown, at both ends of each strap to fix them securely in place.

7 To make the large flower, fold each of the five check fabric squares in half to form a rectangle then fold down both top corners to the bottom center to form a triangle as shown. Lay all five triangles next to each other in a line and work a running stitch along the bottom edge. Do not knot off the end of the thread because you need to gather.

Fold over

Fold to center

8 Gather from both ends of the thread, pushing all the petals as close together as possible. Tie both ends of the thread together. Arrange the petals so that they overlap and stitch in place to secure. Repeat Steps 7 and 8 with the orange silk fabric squares to create the small flower.

Pull both ends and tighten

Pull thread

9 To embellish the center of the flower take half a long zipper and work a running stitch down the length. Do not tie a knot in the ends of the thread because you need to gather the zipper so that it coils up. When the zip is coiled stitch randomly to secure in place. Use the hot glue gun to attach the small flower onto the large flower, with the coiled zipper in the center. Then use the glue gun to stick the flower onto the bag. Add a coordinating button to the center of the coiled zipper if desired.

CHAPTER 3

Pretty Decorations

This chapter of zesty and bright projects will brighten up the darker corners of your motorhome, caravan, or campervan. Making a feature of the more practical and built-in items in your space will give them an individual look that is often hard to achieve within the barriers of a temporary space. Jazz up shelving units with a crochet trim or get creative by repurposing glass jars for storage—there are no limits to your imagination.

Crochet bunting

Create this gorgeous granny triangle bunting with its funky
neon pink sequin trim—it's sure to get you noticed.

WHAT TO DO

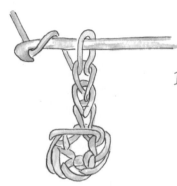

1 Using green yarn,
make a chain of 4
stitches and join
with slip stitch
into a circle. **Round
1:** Working into the
circle, chain 3.

2 Work 2 double crochet, chain 3, 3
double crochet, chain 3, 3 double
crochet, chain 3, join to the top
chain of the first 3-chain with a
slip stitch.

NOTE
US and UK crochet patterns share stitch names
but these do not refer to the same stitches.
This crochet pattern is written using US crochet
terminology. See pages 133–135 for details of
how to work each stitch.
Single crochet (US) = double crochet (UK)
Double crochet (US) = treble crochet (UK)

3 Change to turquoise. **Round 2:** Chain 3, 2 double
crochet, chain 3, 3 double crochet (into corner
space) chain 1, 3 double crochet, chain 3, 3
double crochet into the next chain-3 space, chain
1, 3 double crochet, chain 3, 3 double crochet
into next chain-3 space, chain 1, join to the top
chain of the first 3-chain with a slip stitch.

4 Change to gray. **Round 3:** Chain 3, 2 double crochet, chain 3, 3 double crochet (into a corner space), chain 1, 3 double crochet into next space, chain 1, 3 double crochet, chain 3, 3 double crochet into next corner, chain 1, 3 double crochet into next chain space, chain 1, 3 double crochet, chain 3, 3 double crochet into next corner, chain 1, 3 double crochet into next space, chain 1, join to the top of the first 3-chain with a slip stitch.

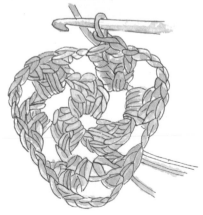

5 Alternating yarn colors, continue working in the same pattern for Rounds 4, 5, 6, 7, 8. Thread 23 sequins onto the gray yarn. **Round 9** (sequin trim): Flip your triangle over and starting in a space, chain 3, 1 double crochet, on the next double crochet work half the stitch.

Just one thing...

These instructions will make a string of bunting around 7 ft (220 cm) in length. To make the bunting longer, just make more triangle flags— although you will need more sequins and yarn.
   You can use beads instead of sequins in the border, but choose lightweight plastic beads rather than glass, which might make the flags too heavy to hang nicely.

6 On the second yarn over trap a sequin into the stitch and then pull the hook through to secure in place.

7 Work 2 double crochet and 1 single crochet into the center stitch of the cluster of double crochet below. Then 5 double crochet (hooking a sequin on second yarn over of third stitch). Keep working around the triangle in this way back to the start, join to the top of the first 3-chain with a slip stitch.

8 Make 8 more triangles, varying the order of the colors: 3 with green centers, 3 with turquoise centers, 3 with gray centers. Sew all the ends in, trim the excess and iron the triangles flat (use a dishtowel to protect the sequins from the heat).

9 Using cream yarn, chain 50 for the end tie. Attach the tie to the first bunting flag by working a slip stitch into the third double crochet of the corner scallop.

pretty decorations

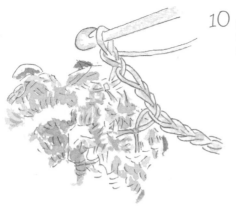

10 For the picot edging, chain 5, slip stitch into the double between the scallops. Repeat along the side of one triangle.

11 Chain 20 for the next section of bunting tie and then attach the chain to the next bunting flag as in step 9. Repeat Step 10 along the top of the next triangle, Repeat these steps to join all nine flags. Make a chain of 50 to complete the tie at the other end.

Crochet shelf edge

Make a feature of those boring shelf edges with this simple but colorful fabric and crochet trim.

GATHER TOGETHER

Strip of fabric the length of the shelf by 2¾ in. (7 cm) wide for each shelf

Sewing needle and thread

Oddments of crochet yarn in green, pink, and yellow

US D/3 (3 mm) crochet hook

Narrow ribbon

WHAT TO DO

1 Fold the fabric lengthwise, RS together, and sew along one end and the long side. Turn inside out, tuck the raw edges in and stitch closed. Press flat. Sew blanket stitch along the folded edge with each stitch about ⅜ in. (1 cm) wide.

2 Using green yarn, work 2 single crochet stitches into the edge of each blanket stitch.

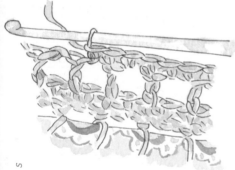

3 At the end of the row, turn the work. Row 1: Chain 1, work 1 single crochet into each stitch to end, turn. Row 2: Chain 4, work [1 double crochet, chain 1] into each alternate stitch to end, turn. Row 3: Chain 1, 1 single crochet into each stitch to end. Break yarn, turn.

4 Join in pink yarn. Row 4: Chain 1, work 1 single crochet into each stitch along row. Break yarn, join in yellow yarn, turn. Begin working the scalloped edging. Row 5: *3 single crochet, chain 3, skip 3 stitches and in fourth stitch work 1 double crochet, chain 3, 1 double crochet into same stitch as previous double crochet, chain 3, skip 3 stitches; repeat sequence from * along row, turn.

pretty decorations

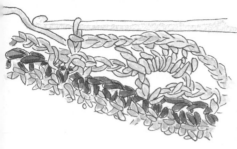

5 Continue in yellow yarn.

Row 6: *1 single crochet in center stitch of 3-single crochet in previous row, chain 3, 7 double crochet in chain-3 in previous row, chain 3; repeat sequence from * along row. Fasten off by pulling the yarn end through the last stitch.

6 Block the crochet trim by pinning to an ironing board and steam ironing the reverse. Thread ribbon through the trellis created on Row 2. Attach to the shelf with pretty pins or double sided tape.

NOTE
US and UK crochet patterns share stitch names but these do not refer to the same stitches. This crochet pattern is written using US crochet terminology. See pages 133–135 for details of how to work each stitch.
Single crochet (US) = double crochet (UK)
Double crochet (US) = treble crochet (UK)

Cross-stitch picture

A whimsical little caravan cross-stitch with pretty ribbon embroidery, which would look gorgeous in a retro camper or caravan.

GATHER TOGETHER

6¼ in. (16 cm) embroidery hoop

8 x 8 in. (20 x 20 cm) Aida cross-stitch fabric

Anchor pearl cotton (size 8) in lemon, coral, raspberry, pink, green, nude, and white

Tapestry needle

6 x 6 in. (15 x 15 cm) piece of Bondaweb

Vintage embroidered tray cloth

Selection of silk ribbons in coordinating colors

Selection of beads and sequins in coordinating colors

1⅜ yd (1.25 m) lemon organza ribbon

1⅛ yd (1 m) white satin ribbon

10 in. (25 cm) lemon bias binding

10 in. (25 cm) narrow coral silk ribbon

WHAT TO DO

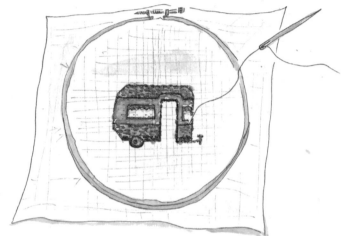

1 Follow the chart on page 138 to work the cross-stitch caravan design onto the Aida fabric, using the embroidery hoop to keep the fabric taut.

2 Trim the fabric down leaving a ¾ in. (2 cm) border around the design. Apply Bondaweb to the back following the manufacturer's instructions and fix the design to a suitable area of the vintage tray cloth.

3 Cut small areas of floral embroidery from the leftover tray cloth. Apply Bondaweb to the back of each piece and arrange around the cross-stitch design to blend the edges of the Aida fabric with the base fabric.

4 Use a selection of silk ribbons to work simple ribbon embroidery stitches (see page 130) around the vintage embroidery.

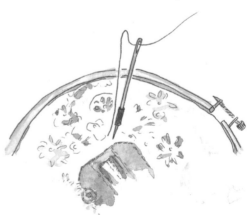

5 Embellish the ribbon embroidery by stitching on assorted beads and sequins, as desired.

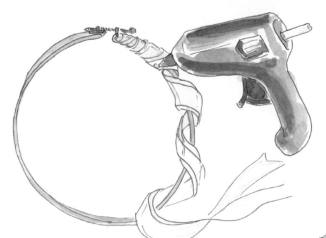

6 Cut 10 in. (25 cm) off the lemon organza ribbon. Layer the longer piece with the white satin ribbon and wrap both around the embroidery frame. Use a hot glue gun to secure in place at regular intervals.

7 Place the lining fabric behind the picture, insert both layers into the embroidery hoop and tighten it up. Trim away excess fabric from the back of the hoop and use the glue gun to hold the raw edges down to neaten.

8 Fold the lemon bias binding in half and use the glue gun to attach either end onto the back of the embroidery hoop at the top edge to make a hanging loop.

9 Tie a bow in the remaining lemon organza ribbon and another in the coral silk ribbon. Use the hot glue gun to attach both to the top of the embroidery hoop.

cross-stitch picture

Glass jar storage

At last—a stylish use for all those glass jars you have been saving. This project doubles the amount of storage offered by a single shelf and is a great place to keep treats for all the family.

GATHER TOGETHER

4 in. (10 cm) squares 4 different patterned fabrics

Pinking shears

4 matching glass jars

Hot glue gun

20 in. (50 cm) blue pompom trimming (or as required to fit glass jar covers)

20 in. (50 cm) pink pompom trimming (or as required to fit glass jar covers)

2¼ yd (2 m) garden twine

3 different glass jars

24 in. (60 cm) whitewashed shelf unit

9 small screws plus screwdriver

3 brown card tags

3⅛ x 6¼ in. (8 x 16 cm) rectangles of 8 different fabrics

1⅛ yd (1 m) lemon bias binding

1⅛ yd (1 m) white cotton trimming

1⅛ yd (1 m) baby rick rack trim

WHAT TO DO

1 Use pinking shears to cut a circle from each of the four patterned fabrics to fit over the lid of the four matching jars. Use a hot glue gun to secure the fabric onto the top and around the edge of the lid.

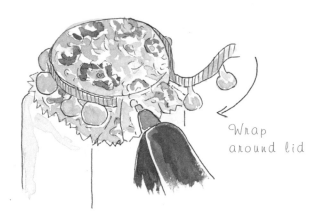

Wrap around lid

2 Glue either blue or pink pompom trimming around the edge of each lid using the hot glue gun. Wrap garden twine around each lid and tie in a bow.

3 Underneath the shelf, mark with a pencil where to place the remaining three lids, spacing them an equal distance apart. Fix the lids to the underside of the shelf by screwing three small screws through each one into the wooden shelf.

4 Cut a length of garden twine and thread it through a brown card tag. Tie the twine around the top of the jar and then screw the jar back onto its matching lid. Repeat for each of the jars.

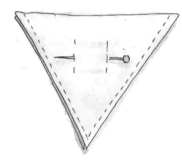

5 To make the baby bunting trim, fold a rectangle of one of the eight different fabrics in half and draw a triangle. Cut through both layers to create a front and back piece. Repeat for the other seven fabrics.

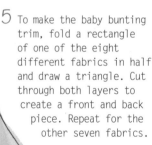

6 With RS together, pin the front and back of each triangle pair together and machine stitch around the sides leaving the top open. Turn RS out and press. Repeat for the other triangle flags.

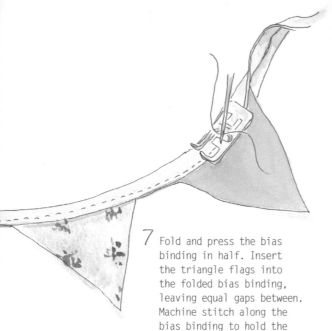

7 Fold and press the bias binding in half. Insert the triangle flags into the folded bias binding, leaving equal gaps between. Machine stitch along the bias binding to hold the flags in place.

8 Use the hot glue gun to attach the white cotton trimming along the shelf edge. Fix the mini bunting on top and the mini rick rack trim on top of that to complete the design. Decorate only the front edge of the shelf or continue around the sides if you wish (you may need more flags.)

Just one thing...

If the bunting trimming is likely to get dirty easily, it would be better to fix it to the shelf with decorative pins rather than glue so it can be removed easily for laundering.
   The jars under the shelf do not have to be identical, but they should all be of a similar size.

Fabric clock

*An unbreakable, practical yet pretty fabric clock,
which is based on a recycled embroidery hoop.*

GATHER TOGETHER

10 in. (25 cm) embroidery
  hoop

2¾ yd (2.5 m) ribbon or
  binding for wrapping the
  frame

Hot glue gun

5 in. (12 cm) square of
  Bondaweb

5 in. (12 cm) square of pink
  silk fabric

Iron

Scissors

Number templates on page 139

4 squares of white felt,
  each measuring 2½ in.
  (6 cm)

Pinking shears

12 in. (30 cm) square piece
  of floral fabric

12 in. (30 cm) square piece
  of lining fabric

8 coordinating buttons

8 white decorative lace/
  crochet circles cut from
  trimming

Matching sewing thread

Selection of beads and
  sequins for decoration

Clock mechanism

16 in. (40 cm) ribbon for
  hanging the clock

WHAT TO DO

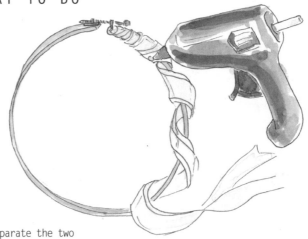

1 Separate the two
  circles of the
  embroidery hoop and wrap the outer frame with the long
  length of ribbon until the frame is completely covered.
  Secure the ribbon at intervals using the hot glue gun.

2 Apply Bondaweb to the back
  of the pink silk following
  the manufacturer's
  instructions. Use the
  templates to draw a 3, 6,
  9, and 12 onto the silk
  and cut out. Peel away the
  Bondaweb backing and iron
  one number onto each white
  felt square. Use pinking
  shears to trim around the edge
  of each square.

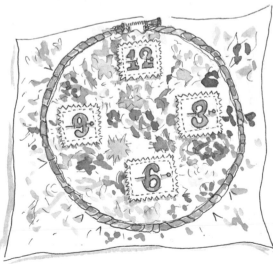

3 Position the floral fabric in the embroidery hoop as desired and tighten the outer ring slightly. Pin the number patches onto the circle to make a clock face. Remove the fabric from the frame and machine stitch the felt number patches in place.

Just one thing...

Don't position the number squares too close to the edge of the circle because when the fabric is finally stretched into place they may be pulled too far off the edge of the clock.

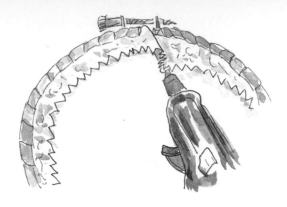

4 Place the floral fabric on top of the lining fabric and put both pieces back into the hoop, with the screw mechanism above the number 12. Tighten the frame as taut as possible. Using pinking shears, trim the excess fabric away from the back and use the hot glue gun to stick the edges down neatly on the back of the frame.

5 Position the eight buttons on top of a lace or crochet circle and hand stitch between the four numbers. Add beads, sequins, and small buttons as extra decoration.

6 Outline each silk number with a line of back stitch for extra definition.

7 Pierce a hole in the center of the clock face and insert the clock mechanism, using the glue gun to secure it to the back of the fabric. Screw the pointers/hands onto the front of the clock.

8 Thread the ribbon through the loop on top of the clock mechanism for extra stability, and then tie it around the screw at the top of the circular frame. Knot the ribbon ends at the desired length. Use the hot glue gun to add extra beads or sequins to the clock.

Fabric bulletin board

Jazz up the caravan—or your home workspace—with this funky fabric and ribbon-embellished bulletin board.

WHAT TO DO

1 Measure the width and height of the cork area inside the frame and add an extra ¼ in. (5 mm) onto each measurement. Cut the main base fabric to this size. Fold under ¼ in. (5 mm) to the WS on all edges and iron flat.

2 Cut a strip from the contrast pocket fabric the same overall width as the base fabric and the desired depth of the pocket. Fold under ¼ in. (5 mm) to the WS on all edges and iron flat. Stitch a piece of crochet lace trim along the top of the pocket edge.

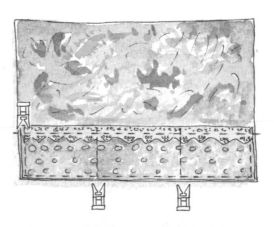

3 Attach the strip to the bottom of the base piece by stitching along the two short sides and the bottom. To create the pockets, stitch two parallel lines 5 in. (18 cm) apart.

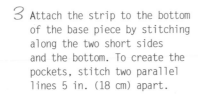

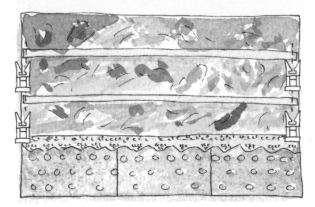

4 Cut two pieces of ribbon the same width as the base fabric. Position one about 3 in. (7.5 cm) from the top and the other equally between it and the top of the pocket. Stitch across each end of the ribbon at the edge of the base fabric.

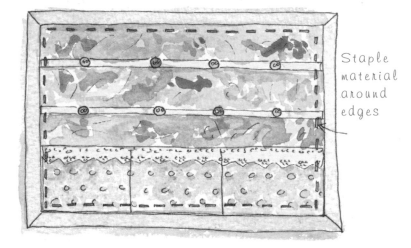

Staple material around edges

5 Position four buttons about 4 in. (10 cm) apart along each ribbon. Using embroidery floss (thread,) sew the buttons through to the base fabric. Staple the edges of the base fabric to the cork board as close the frame as possible.

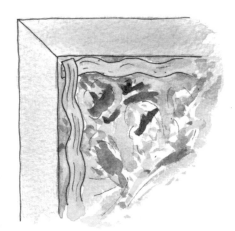

6 Cut the rick rack into two lengths the inside frame width and two lengths the inside frame height. Glue the rick rack around inside the frame to cover the staples.

Just one thing...

For a zingy effect, match the color of the rick rack braid to one of the less obvious colors in the main fabric design so it creates a line of bright contrast around the border.

Dreamcatcher

Breathe new life into a vintage doily by making it into this irresistibly pretty dreamcatcher.

GATHER TOGETHER

¼ oz (10 g) cotton yarn in each of pink, yellow, lilac, green, and turquoise

Inner ring of an embroidery hoop approximately the same diameter as the doily

Crochet doily

Sewing needle and thread

5 pieces of fabric, each 8 x 8 in. (20 x 20 cm)

5 pieces of Bondaweb, each 3¼ x 8 in. (8 x 20 cm)

Scissors

Iron

Template on page 139

Sequins and beads

12 in. (30 cm) ribbon

WHAT TO DO

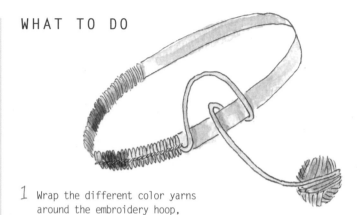

1 Wrap the different color yarns around the embroidery hoop, knotting in place as illustrated, until all the wood is covered.

2 Place the doily onto the reverse of the hoop and stitch to the yarn wrapped around the hoop, using sewing thread.

3 For the fabric feathers, cut a fabric piece in half and iron a piece of Bondaweb to the WS of one half, following the manufacturer's instructions. Place the other half on top WS together and iron again to fix the layers. Place the feather template from page 139 on top and cut a feather shape. Repeat with the other fabrics to make five different feathers.

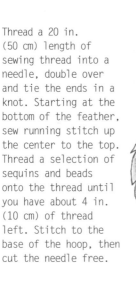

4 Thread a 20 in. (50 cm) length of sewing thread into a needle, double over and tie the ends in a knot. Starting at the bottom of the feather, sew running stitch up the center to the top. Thread a selection of sequins and beads onto the thread until you have about 4 in. (10 cm) of thread left. Stitch to the base of the hoop, then cut the needle free.

5 Repeat Step 4 another four times, twice with 12 in. (30 cm) lengths of thread on either side of the first feather, and twice with 16 in. (40 cm) lengths on the outside edges.

6 Cut slits evenly spaced along both sides of all fabric feathers, stopping approximately ¼ in. (5 mm) from the center stitching, to create that twisted effect. Thread the ribbon through the top of the hoop and tie in a bow to complete.

Upcycled vintage plates

A brilliantly quirky way to upcycle mismatched plates into funky wall art. Use the templates given or create your own design.

WHAT TO DO

1 Trace the outline of your chosen design onto a piece of paper, enlarge on a photocopier if necessary, and cut out neatly. Apply glue to one side of the paper template and carefully position in place on the plate. Choose an area where the pattern of the original plate will show through once the paper is removed.

2 Spread out newsprint in a well ventilated area, preferably outside, and shake the can of spray paint well. Spray the plate with an even layer of paint and leave to dry, according to the manufacturer's instructions.

3 Carefully peel away the paper template (the glue stick allows a little hold but comes away easily) to reveal your design.

Peel away template

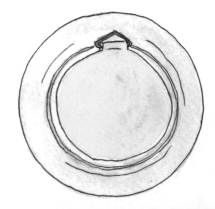

4 Complete by attaching the self-adhesive plate hanger to the back of the plate at the top. Repeat steps for the other plates and designs. Display your plates in a group on a wall, or in a row above a window.

Lavender "tea" bags

These charming scented bags are made to look like tea sachets, complete with tags. Too pretty to hide, hang them to scent the room.

GATHER TOGETHER

4 pieces of pink organza fabric, each 4 x 5½ in. (10 x 14 cm)

4 pieces of pale yellow netting, each 4 x 5½ in. (10 x 14 cm)

Matching sewing threads

Sewing machine

2 teaspoons dried lavender

Hot glue gun

8 in. (20 cm) each of orange and lilac trimming

8 in. (20 cm) pale yellow bias binding

8 in. (20 cm) pink trimming

8 in. (20 cm) each of pink and green spotted ribbon

12 in. (30 cm) pink rick rack trim

12 in. (30 cm) blue cord

4 1½ in. (4 cm) squares of floral paper

Assorted coordinating buttons

WHAT TO DO

1 Take two pieces of organza fabric and place one on top of the other. Place a piece of netting on either side of the organza and pin all four pieces together. Repeat with the other pieces.

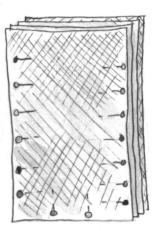

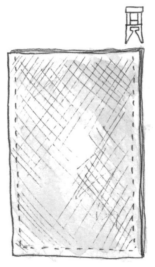

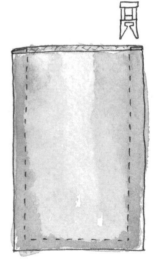

2 Machine stitch around the bottom and side edges of both sets of fabric layers using a French seam: with WS together stitch the first seam ½ in. (1 cm) from the raw edge and then trim to ⅛ in. (3 mm). Turn WS out and press the seam on the fold. Now machine stitch again, ⅛ in. (3 mm) inside the original stitching line.

3 To make the "base" of
the bag, flatten both
bottom corners to form two
triangles. Pin in place
and then stitch across the
corner. Turn the bag RS out
and press the side seams.

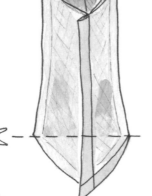

4 Place a teaspoon of dried lavender in each bag, fold the
top edge of the bag over, and pin. Machine stitch across
the top to hold the lavender in place. Use a hot glue gun
or stitching to add trimmings and bias binding to finish
the top of the bag. Secure one end of a length of rick
rack trim or cord to the top of the bag.

5 For the "tea sachet" tags,
use pinking shears to cut two
paper squares. Use the hot
glue gun to stick the pieces
together back to back, with
the other end of the rick
rack trim or cord caught
between them. Add buttons for
further decoration. Repeat to
make second tag and tie both
lavender bags together.

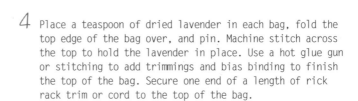

Pompom garland

Create a fun pompom and felt ball garland to brighten up a dull corner or add a splash of color to your outdoor space.

GATHER TOGETHER

Pompom template on page 137

Cardstock (cardboard)—from old cereal boxes is ideal

Scissors

5 x 1 oz (25 g) balls of yarn in assorted colors

¾ oz (20 g) wool tops in 5 assorted colors

J-cloth

Dishwashing liquid

Jug or spray bottle

8 in. (20 cm) piece of bubble wrap

Butcher's twine

Large-eyed needle

WHAT TO DO

1 Using the template on page 137, cut out 20 donut shapes in cardstock to create 10 pairs. To make the wrapping process easier, cut lengths of yarn approximately 79 in. (2 m) long and wind into smaller balls. Start to wrap the yarn around the donut-shaped card templates, starting at the back of the rings and passing the yarn through the center. Keep wrapping until the hole in the middle is nearly full, adding new lengths of yarn as you go.

Wrap

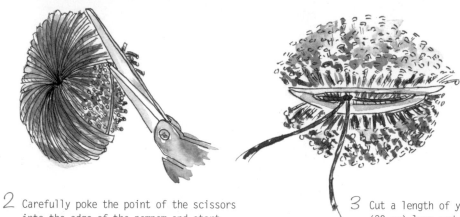

2 Carefully poke the point of the scissors into the edge of the pompom and start cutting around the edge until you can see the edge of the cardstock. Then slide the scissors between the two layers of cardstock and carry on cutting until you have cut through all the loops of yarn. Do not pull the cardstock template out at this stage.

3 Cut a length of yarn 12 in. (30 cm) long and tie around the middle of the pompom between the cardstock layers. Pull tightly and tie in a double knot. Do not trim the yarn ends as you will need them to attach the pompoms to the garland.

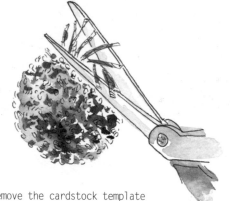

4 Remove the cardstock template by carefully easing the rings apart. Fluff the pompom up, trimming off any loose or longer threads. Make nine more pompoms in the same way in the colors of your choice and put to one side.

5 Place a small piece of wool top in the middle of a J-cloth. Lay further wool top round it until you have a large ball of wool tops, approximately 8 in. (20 cm) in diameter. Mix a small amount of warm water with a squeeze of dishwashing liquid in a jug or spray bottle and dampen the ball of wool tops slightly. Take the ball in one hand and gently start to roll it between both hands. Do not apply much pressure at this point; the slower you start the less likely the felt will crack. Continue to roll until the ball starts to felt; it will suddenly feel smaller and harder.

Roll

6 At this point start using the texture side of the bubble wrap, which adds more friction so the ball will felt more quickly. After 5-10 minutes of rolling your ball will be felted and ready to use.

7 Make nine more balls in the same way. Try to use the same amount of wool top each time for balls the same size.

8 Cut a piece of butchers' twine 100 in. (2.5 m) long. Working from the center outward, thread a felt ball onto the twine and tie a knot either side to keep it in place. Using the yarn ends, tie a pompom tightly further along the twine. Keep alternating felt balls and pompoms until your garland is ready to hang!

CHAPTER 4

Outdoor Living

The best part of glamping is spending time in the fresh air with friends and family! This section of the book concentrates on projects to enhance your time outside and make sure you enjoy it in style. Relax in a vintage-style deck chair, picnic on a stunning crochet blanket, or watch the sunset surrounded by twinkling lights in pretty handcrafted holders. We were inspired by traditional seaside holidays—pastel ice-cream colors, striped fabrics, and retro themes run throughout the chapter. Whether the sun is shining or there is a touch of frost in the air, you can make the most of your precious time outside in crafted heaven!

Fabric checkerboard

A simple fabric checkerboard that can be laminated to ensure it will withstand the wettest and windiest of summer days!

GATHER TOGETHER

8½ x 16½ in. (22 x 42 cm) piece of Bondaweb

8½ x 16½ in. (22 x 42 cm) piece of patterned fabric

Iron

Scissors

16½ in. (42 cm) square of plain or dotted fabric

16½ in. (42 cm) square of fusible plastic sheet

70 in. (176 cm) bias binding

16½ in. (42 cm) square of base fabric

Sewing machine

Oven-bake clay

Rolling pin

Butterfly stamp

Bottle top (or round cutter)

Pink and green paint

Paintbrushes

Pearlescent cream paint

Clear craft varnish

WHAT TO DO

1 Iron the Bondaweb to the WS of the patterned fabric, following the manufacturer's instructions. Draw a 2 in. (5 cm) grid onto the Bondaweb backing. Cut out all 32 squares.

2 Use a ruler and pencil to draw a grid, 8 x 8 squares, onto the plain or dotted fabric. Peel the backing off the 32 squares and iron in place on the grid in a checkerboard pattern. Place the fusible plastic sheet over the checkerboard and fix it in place, following the manufacturer's instructions.

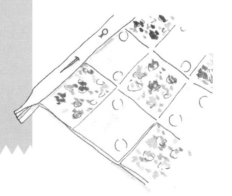

3 Cut the bias binding into four 17½ in. (44 cm) strips, fold the strips in half lengthwise and press. Place the checkerboard top onto the backing fabric, WS together, and fold a length of bias binding over one edge. Pin in place.

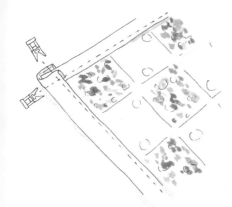

4 At the first corner, tuck the ends of the binding under, level with the end, to neaten. Fold the ends of the following strip under and overlap the previous strip. Repeat on the other corners, overlapping the start strip over the fourth strip. Machine stitch around to attach the binding.

5 Roll out the clay to ¼ in. (5 mm) thick. Stamp 16 butterfly imprints into the clay. Cut out into disks using the bottle top. If using oven-bake clay, put the checkers into the oven to harden.

6 Paint eight checkers with pink paint and eight with green—or use alternative colors to match your color theme. Add a coat of pearlescent cream paint and another of clear varnish to finish.

Funky flowers shower cap

Create this waterproof retro shower cap to add a touch
of glamour to your beauty regime.

GATHER TOGETHER

20 x 20 in. (50 x 50 cm)
  piece of cotton fabric

Iron

Sequins

Scissors

1 yd (1 m) Vilene Lamifix
  Matte

7 pieces of cotton fabric,
  each 10 x 4 in. (25 x 10 cm)

Flower templates on page 141

Sewing machine

Matching sewing thread

Hand-sewing needle

2¼ yd (2 m) pale blue bias
  binding

1 yd (1 m) elastic

WHAT TO DO

1 Iron the large
  piece of fabric and
  sprinkle on a thin
  layer of sequins. Cut
  the Lamifix in half,
  place one piece over
  the fabric and follow
  the manufacturer's
  instructions to bond
  the layers. Let cool,
  then cut an 18 in.
  (45 cm) diameter
  circle from the
  sequined fabric.

2 Iron the remaining Lamifix onto
  the smaller pieces of fabric,
  omitting the sequins. Using the
  templates, draw one large, one
  medium and one small flower
  on the laminated fabrics and
  cut out. Layer the flowers
  with one of each size, mixing
  and matching fabrics. Pin
  the flowers onto the sequined
  circle and machine stitch a
  circle in the center of each
  flower to attach.

Fold
over

3 Open out the bias binding. With RS facing and
  edges aligned, machine stitch one edge of the
  bias binding around the edge of the shower cap.

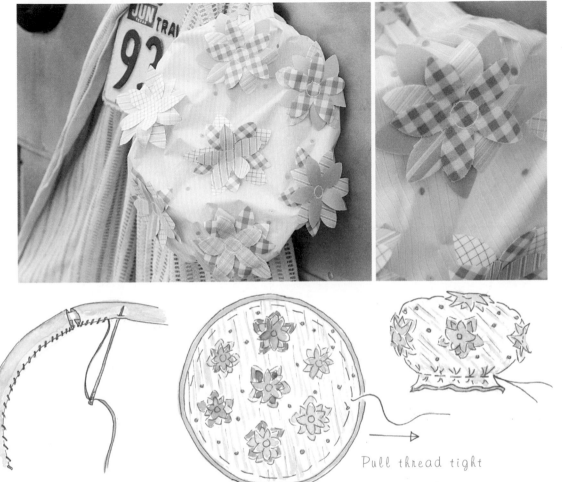

Pull thread tight

4 Fold the bias binding over to the WS and stitch in place by hand, using small neat hem stitches.

5 Make a long running stitch around the cap, about 1½ in. (4 cm) from the edge. Pull the threads to gather the fabric to fit your head. Tie the threads and even out the gathers around the hat.

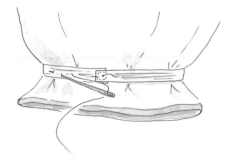

6 Wrap the elastic around your head—don't stretch it—to determine the length needed, then add ¾ in. (2 cm). Cut, overlap the ends, and stitch together. Place the ring of elastic over the running stitch on the WS of the hat. Stitch the elastic to the inside of the shower cap using back stitch, then take out the running stitches. Your cap is now ready to use!

Pocket tidy

This smart tidy can be tied to hang or slotted over the back of a chair to keep all those essentials handy.

GATHER TOGETHER

2 strips of dotted fabric (for the pockets) each measuring 31 x 12 in. (78 x 30 cm)

Scissors

Sewing machine

12 x 12 in. (30 x 30 cm) piece of Bondaweb

Templates on page 140

Scraps of floral and plain fabric for the appliqué

Iron

Free-motion embroidery foot

Embroidery floss (thread) and needle

Coordinating buttons

23 x 21 in. (58 x 52 cm) piece of base fabric

46 in. (116 cm) green bias binding

46 in. (116 cm) decorative trimming

23 x 8¼ in. (58 x 21 cm) piece of fabric for hood

23 x 8¼ in. (58 x 21 cm) piece of fabric for hood lining

72 in. (180 cm) white cotton ribbon

23 x 21 in. (58 x 52 cm) piece of backing fabric

WHAT TO DO

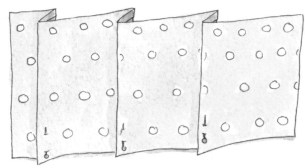

1 Fold under and hem the top edge of each piece of dotted fabric. Make three 2 in. (5 cm) wide pleats spaced across each strip for the pockets. Press and pin in place.

2 Apply the Bondaweb onto the WS of the fabric scraps following the manufacturer's instructions. Cut six flower shapes and 12 leaf shapes, remove the paper backing and arrange the shapes onto each pocket, using the photograph as a guide. Iron in place.

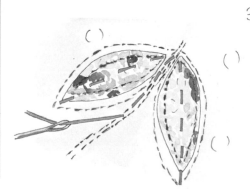

3 Using a free-motion foot attachment on the sewing machine, stitch freely around the flower appliqué. Add hand embroidery (see pages 129-130) and stitch on buttons.

4 With RS up, pin the pocket
strips on the base fabric.
Flip cach pleat open and
machine stitch vertically
down the rear fold to
create separate pockets.
Flip the pleat back and
stitch across the bottom
of each pocket strip.

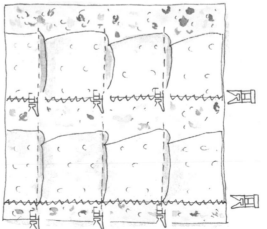

5 Cut the bias binding in half and pin along the bottom edge of each pocket strip; zigzag stitch down the center. Add decorative trimming, using a straight machine stitch.

6 Place the hood and hood lining RS together. Stitch along the bottom edge only then turn RS out. Press the seam out.

Ribbons overlapped

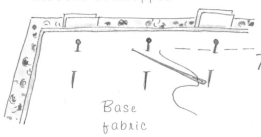

Base fabric

7 Cut the ribbon into six equal lengths. Place the main pocket panel RS up and pin the lengths of ribbon in pairs at the center and at each end of the top edge. Place the hood on top RS down with raw edges aligned. Tack along the top edge.

8 Place the backing fabric RS down on top of all layers and machine stitch around all edges and through all layers, leaving a gap along the top edge for turning. Trim all seams, remove tacking stitches, turn RS out and press.

9 Fold, press and machine stitch along the top edge to close the opening. The pocket tidy can now be either tied and hung or placed over the back of a chair.

Just one thing...

Make sure you arrange the layers of pocket panel, ribbons, hood and lining exactly as described in Steps 6 to 8 so that when the pocket tidy is turned RS outward everything will be in the correct place.

If you don't want to tackle appliqué and machine embroidery to decorate the pockets, make up a layered fabric and felt flower for each pocket instead—see pages 34-35. Alternatively you could stitch on decorative buttons, beads or sequins to create your own interesting design.

Embroidered towel

Keep your valuables safe in the sun with the handy
pockets in this appliqué beach hut towel.

GATHER TOGETHER

2 matching bath sheets

Pillow

Scissors

11 x 14 in. (27.5 x 35 cm)
  piece of fabric

2¼ yd (2 m) crochet lace
  trim

Sewing machine and thread

Fabric for binding

Templates on page 140

Scraps of fabric for
  appliqué

Bondaweb

Iron

Buttons

Embroidery floss (thread)

1¾ yd (1.5 m) rick rack
  trim

1¾ yd (1.5 m) ribbon

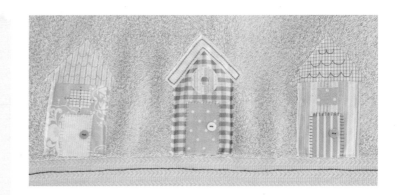

WHAT TO DO

1 Wrap one bath sheet
  loosely around the
  pillow and trim
  the length to
  fit, allowing
  an extra 1 in.
  (2.5 cm) on each end.
  Mark the two pockets, using
  the illustration below as a guide, and then
  remove the terrycloth piece from the pillow.

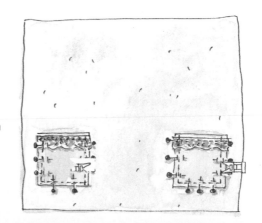

2 Cut 2 pieces of fabric 11 x 7 in.
  (27.5 x 17.5 cm) for the pockets.
  Press the edges under all around
  each piece by ⅜ in. (1 cm). Pin
  and then machine stitch a piece of
  the crochet lace to the top of each
  pocket. Stitch the pockets to the
  terrycloth using the marks made in
  step 1 as a guide.

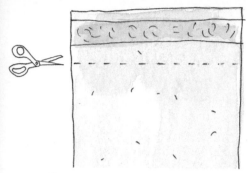

3 Cut one end off the second bath sheet, just below the decorative woven strip if it has one.

4 Cut two strips of the binding fabric 1 in. (2.5 cm) wide and as long as the sides of the main terrycloth piece (You may have to join strips). Cut another two strips 1 in. (2.5 cm) wide and as long as the sides of the pillow piece. Press under the long edges on each strip, then fold in half lengthwise and use to bind the edges of both pieces of terrycloth.

5 Fold the pillow piece in half with pockets RS out. Place pocket side up on the main terrycloth piece with raw ends of pillow and main piece aligned and stitch the seam. Turn the entire piece over, folding the pillow right over to lie on the top of the other side, and stitch the seam again. This encloses the raw edges in a French seam.

6 Use the template on page 141 to cut the main hut shapes from fabric. Copy the window, door, roof and ring details onto the paper backing of the Bondaweb. Cut out the shapes and iron to the assorted appliqué fabrics. Peel the backing from the Bondaweb and iron the details onto each beach hut, following the manufacturer's instructions. Decorate with embroidery and sew on a small button for each door handle.

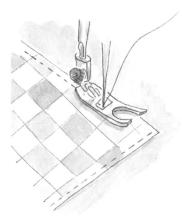

7 Arrange the beach huts evenly
spaced in a line across the
bottom of the towel and pin in
place. Stitch around the edges
of each to secure, using a
sewing machine.

8 Sew crochet lace to the edge
of the bottom of the towel,
tucking the ends underneath.
Sew a row of vertical straight
stitches above the lace,
stitch a piece of ribbon above
that, then add a strip of rick
rack and finally embroider a
row of chain stitch. Insert
the pillow into the pocket and
your sunbathing towel is ready
for use!

Glass jar lanterns

Turn old preserve or condiment jars into cute and colorful lanterns with this easy project.

WHAT TO DO

GATHER TOGETHER

Scraps of fabric

Scissors

Craft glue

3 old glass jars, cleaned and with the paper labels soaked off

3¼ yd (3 m) 1 mm jewelry wire, cut into 3 equal lengths

Selection of beads and sequins

Battery-operated tea lights

1 Cut the fabric into ½ x 8 in. (1 x 20 cm) strips. Dilute the craft glue with a little water and dip the strips to coat with glue. Rub off excess glue and then line the inside of the jar with vertical strips of fabric. Repeat with the other jars and leave to dry overnight.

2 Trim any excess fabric around the neck of the jar. Wrap a piece of wire around the neck and twist the end to secure, making sure it is fairly tight because it will be part of the handle.

3 Thread beads and sequins onto the wire: 8-12 in. (20-30 cm) of beaded handle is about right. Twist the remaining wire through the neck wire to hold the handle in place.

Wrap wire under

Wrap wire around

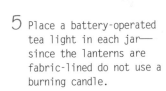

4 Thread a couple of beads or sequins onto the end of the wire and then thread the wire end over the neck wire. Keep adding beads or sequins and threading the wire over all round the neck. Cut off excess wire.

5 Place a battery-operated tea light in each jar—since the lanterns are fabric-lined do not use a burning candle.

Seaside crochet blanket

Whether basking in the sunshine or snuggling up against the
sea breeze, this cozy crochet blanket is ideal.

WHAT TO DO

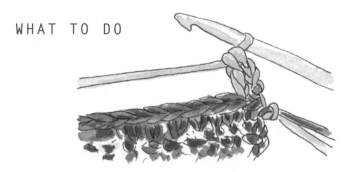

1 Using coral yarn, make a chain of 206 stitches. **Row 1:** Work 1
half double crochet into the third chain from the hook, 1 half
double crochet into each stitch to end, turn. **Row 2:** Chain 2,
1 half double crochet into each stitch to end, turn. Repeat
Row 2 four more times. Join in green yarn. **Row 7:** Chain 3,
work 1 double crochet into the first stitch.

2 *Skip 2 stitches, work 3 double crochet into
next stitch; rep from * to last stitch, work 2
double crochet into last stitch, turn.

NOTE

US and UK crochet patterns
share stitch names but these
do not refer to the same
stitches. This crochet pattern
is written using US crochet
terminology. See pages
133–135 for details of how
to work each stitch.

Single crochet (US) =
double crochet (UK)

Half double crochet (US) =
half treble crochet (UK)

Double crochet (US) = treble
crochet (UK)

3 Join in blue yarn. **Row 8:** Chain 2, work 1 half double crochet into each stitch to end, turn. **Row 9:** Chain 3, work 1 double crochet into each of second and third stitches.

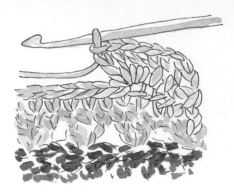

4 Work 5 double crochet into the next stitch.

5 Slip the hook out of the top of the last double crochet, insert it into the top of the first double crochet.

6 Then insert the hook back into the loop again and pull it through (1 bobble made).

7 *Work 1 double crochet into each of the next 5 stitches, then repeat steps 4 to 6 to create another bobble; rep from * to last 3 stitches, work 1 double crochet into each of last 3 stitches, turn. **Row 10:** Chain 2, work 1 half double crochet into each stitch to the end, turn.

8 Join in cream yarn. **Row 11:** Chain 3, work 1 double crochet into first stitch. *Skip 2 stitches, work 3 double crochet into next stitch; rep from * to last stitch, work 2 double crochets into last stitch, turn.

9 Join in pink yarn. **Row 12:** Chain 3, work 3 double crochet into the first gap between clusters of the row below. Continue working clusters of 3 double crochet into each gap between clusters to the end.

10 On the last double crochet, chain 3 and attach to the top of the double crochet below, turn.

11 Join in lilac yarn. **Row 13:** Chain 3, work 1 double crochet into the first stitch. *Skip 3 stitches, work 3 double crochet into gap between clusters; rep from * to last stitch, work 2 double crochet into last stitch, turn. **Row 14:** Rep Row 12 in pink. **Row 15:** Rep Row 13 in cream. (5 rows of granny stripe) Rep Rows 8 to 10 in blue, then Row 7 in green to complete the repeat design of 18 rows.

12 Keep repeating Rows 2 to 19 in the colors as set until your blanket is the desired size. Using coral, rep Rows 2 to 6 once more. Fasten off.

13 To work the edging, join in green and work clusters of 3 double crochet into every third stitch along the top of the blanket.

14 At the corner, work a cluster of 3 double crochet in the corner of the blanket, chain 4, work another cluster of 3 double crochet in the same stitch.

15 Continue around the rest of the blanket in the same way, fasten off. Join in cream, work clusters of 3 double crochet into the gaps of the round below along the whole edge, working 1 cluster, chain 4, 1 cluster into the same gap at each corner.

16 Join in pink. Work a round of single crochet along the whole edge, at each corner working 4 single crochet into the 4-chain space. Using lilac, work a round of half double crochet along the whole edge. Sew in all the ends and trim loose ends.

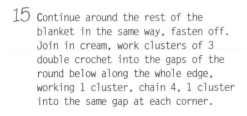

Deck chair

The decoration on this deck chair is a great way to bring memories alive by using photos of family members and favorite vacations.

WHAT TO DO

1 With the deck chair frame flat, measure the length and add on enough extra to fold the fabric over the wooden batons and for a hem at each end. Cut the deck chair fabric to this measurement.

Peel off backing after ironing

2 Use a scanner or color photocopier to copy the postcards or vintage photos onto heat transfer paper, following the manufacturer's instructions. Cut the images out and transfer directly onto the deck chair fabric. Alternatively, transfer the images onto plain muslin and then cut and stitch onto the fabric.

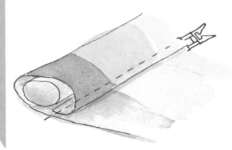

3 Fold over each end of the fabric into a small hem, then fold again to make a channel for the batons. Stitch along the first fold line with the sewing machine.

4 Cut the coral fabric into one strip 18 x 3¼ in. (45 x 8 cm), one strip 13 x 3¼ in. (33 x 8 cm), and two strips each 22¾ x 3¼ in. (58 x 8 cm). Cut the striped fabric into one strip 18 x 6¼ in. (45 x 6 cm), one strip 13 x 6¼ in. (33 x 6 cm), and two strips 22¾ x 6¼ in. (58 x 6 cm). Apply Bondaweb to the back of each strip, following the manufacturer's instructions.

5 Iron the strips to one piece of the muslin to create the Union Jack. Zigzag stitch the orange and blue rick rack onto the diagonals to complete the design. Zigzag along all raw edges and then add the buttons.

6 Place the two pieces of muslin RS together and machine stitch around the sides and bottom, leaving the top open. Turn out and press. Insert the pillow pad.

Just one thing...

Vintage postcards and photos can often be found at yard sales or antique shops if you do not have any of your own. They must be scanned or photocopied onto the transfer paper—you cannot use the originals—so it's fine to use items of sentimental value because the originals will not be damaged.

If you don't want a Union Jack design on your pillow, make up your own design in appliqué or embroidery.

7 Fold the remaining length of deck chair fabric in half. Place the cushion on top, with open raw edges aligned with the raw edges of the flap, and machine stitch together. Press the seam allowance toward the flap. Use the glue gun to fix a length of decorative trim over the seam allowance to hide the raw edges.

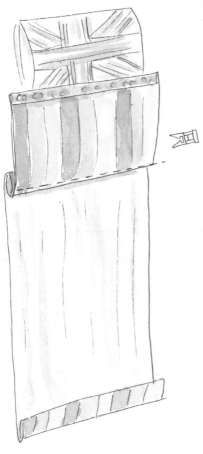

8 Turn the deck chair cover over. Align the fold of the flap on the cushion along the bottom fold of the channel at the top of the deck chair. Machine stitch the flap to the deck chair cover along the existing channel stitching line—the cushion will hang over the front of the deck chair on the flap of fabric. Use the batons to attach the cover onto the deck chair.

Windbreak

Why have a boring windbreak when you can have this decorative design to add a glamorous feel to a day on the beach.

GATHER TOGETHER

2¾ yd (2.5 m) fabric

Sewing machine

Matching sewing thread

4 wooden windbreak posts

14 x 20 in. (35 x 50 cm) piece of Bondaweb

Assorted pieces of fabric for the appliqué

Templates on page 141

11½ in. (28 cm) of trim in each of three different styles/colors

6 in. (15 cm) ribbon

6 in. (15 cm) rick rack trim

8 in. (20 cm) rick rack trim or ribbon in each of 3 different styles/colors

Coordinating embroidery floss (thread) and needle

12 buttons

Selection of sequins

WHAT TO DO

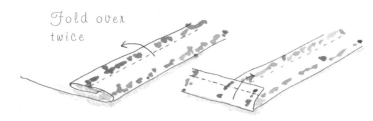

Fold over twice

1 Fold the top and bottom edges of the main fabric over twice to make a double hem and stitch in place. Fold over the ends once by ¼ in. (5 mm) and stitch in place.

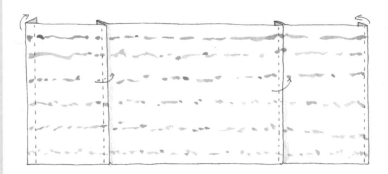

2 Fold each side of the main fabric under by 2 in. (5 cm), or to fit the wooden posts, and pin in place. Machine stitch down to make a channel for the post. Measure 20 in. (50 cm) in from each end and make a 2 in. (5 cm) pleat in the fabric (or a pleat to fit the wooden post). Pin and machine stitch to make the two channels for the remaining posts.

3 Fix Bondaweb onto the back of the fabric pieces for the appliqué, following the manufacturer's instructions. Using the templates on page 141, cut three different pieces of fabric for the beach huts, three different pieces of fabric for the doors, and three triangles in different fabrics for the roofs. Peel away the paper backing on each piece ready to add the beach hut design to the windbreak.

4 Pin the main part of each beach hut onto the center section of the windbreak with a gap of about 2 in. (5 cm) between each one. Pin a triangular roof on each hut. Follow the manufacturer's instructions to bond everything in place.

5 Cut the three circles for the life rings in different fabrics. Cut a hole in the center of each to make a ring. Cut three small triangular flags from different fabrics. Arrange the rings, doors and flags onto the beach huts using the photograph on page 123 as a guide. Bond the pieces in place as before.

6 Pin assorted trimming along the base and sides of each roof. Use one of the trims to add a vertical flagpole at the top of each roof. Machine stitch all the trimmings in place.

7 Work a wide zigzag stitch along the raw edges at sides and base of each beach hut. Zigzag stitch around each door and the flag. Work chain stitch around the life rings. Add long stitches to create a striped effect on the life ring. Add buttons and sequins to the design as desired.

8 Insert a wooden post into each of the four stitched tubes. To store the windbreak, simply roll it up with posts in place.

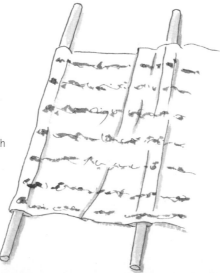

CHAPTER 5

Techniques

Since this book is packed with such an exciting range of different craft techniques we have put together this simple and easy-to-follow section covering the basic techniques featured throughout the projects. There are, however, some more specialist techniques for certain projects, which are explained thoroughly in the relevant step-by-step instructions. Also included are all the templates you will need to complete the projects.

Sewing

Here are a few basic sewing techniques that are used in many of the projects.

BASTING (TACKING)

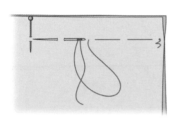

A long, straight stitch, usually made by hand within the seam allowance, used to hold layers in place temporarily during construction but removed after the final seam is stitched. On fine or slippery fabrics the stitches can be made smaller and more even in size.

RUNNING OR GATHERING STITCH

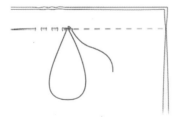

A long, straight stitch made by hand, used to gather fabric or as a decorative stitch. For gathering, the stitches should be fairly loose so they can be drawn up to gather the fabric evenly.

OVERSTITCH (OVERSEW)

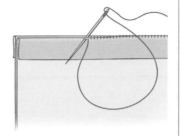

Used to close openings. With the edges together, bring the needle out through one folded edge, pick up a few threads from the other side of the opening and then thread it back into the first folded edge. Continue along the opening, drawing the two sides together as you work.

SLIPSTITCH

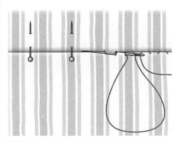

This is used to stitch two layers of fabric together so that the stitches are almost invisible on the right side. Work a stitch along the fold of the fabric, then a tiny stitch on the other layer making sure it doesn't go through to the front surface.

TOPSTITCHING

A row of straight machine stitching added near the edge of a seam or fold. It is often worked in a contrast thread for decorative effect.

SEWING A SEAM

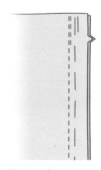

When machine stitching try out the stitch length and the tension on a double layer of scrap fabric first. Make a few reverse stitches to secure the seam at the beginning and end. Stitch along the seam line at an even speed, using the lines on the stitch plate to keep the seam allowance even.

FRENCH SEAM

This is a double seam that encloses the raw edges of the seam allowance. The seam is first stitched with the fabric WS together, then pressed back along itself RS together and the seam stitched again.

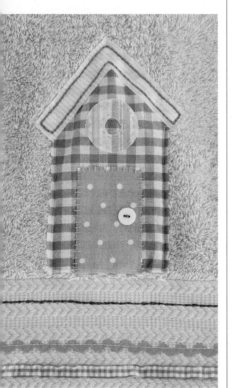

APPLIQUÉ

Appliqué can be used to create motifs and surface decoration. Bondaweb is a quick and easy way to attach the layers together, keeping your design flat ready for further decorative stitching.

1 Trace the outlines of all the different pieces needed to make up the appliqué from the template. Transfer the shapes onto separate areas of the paper backing of a piece of Bondaweb.

2 Cut the Bondaweb tracing into separate pieces.

3 Decide on the color for each part of the design and select the fabrics. Iron a Bondaweb piece onto the wrong side of the corresponding piece of fabric—you can place several pieces on the same fabric as long as they are spaced apart.

4 Cut around the bonded shapes and peel away the paper backing. Build up the design by placing the pieces adhesive side down onto the base fabric. When you are happy with the arrangement, press the pieces in place with a hot iron, following the manufacturer's instructions.

SEWING ON BEADS, SEQUINS, AND BUTTONS

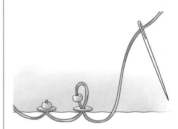

To stitch on a sequin with a bead, bring the thread up through the fabric then thread on the sequin and tiny bead, take the thread over the bead and back down through the hole in the sequin. Single beads are sewn on in the same way, omitting the sequin. To sew on a button, stitch through the holes or through the ring at the back, depending on the button type.

Embroidery

These embroidery stitches are easy to work but very effective.
For more stitches, consult a specialist embroidery book.

BACK STITCH

Back stitch is a very useful stitch because it gives the effect of a continuous line. Bring the thread up through the fabric then work a stitch backwards. Go down through the fabric and underneath, and come up a stitch length in front of the last stitch. Work the next stitch backwards to meet the end of the first stitch worked. Repeat to make a continuous line of stitching.

COUCHING

Basic couching uses two threads, one laid on the fabric surface and a second thread that is stitched over the top to hold the first one down. The two threads can be the same color or different colors. Couching can also be used in beadwork, with the beads threaded onto the first thread and stitches made in the second thread between each bead.

SATIN STITCH

Work straight stitches very close together, working to the outline of the shape and keeping the edges even. You may prefer to draw the shape onto the fabric first; if so, ensure that your stitches are worked to the outside of the line so it does not show.

CHAIN STITCH

This is a great stitch for outlining motifs or shapes within an appliqué design. Take a short stitch in the fabric, and loop the thread around the tip of the needle. To begin the next stitch, take the needle back down into the fabric again at the top of the loop, right next to where the thread emerges.

FRENCH KNOTS

French knots are created by winding the thread around the needle three times before inserting it back into the fabric right next to where it came out. The French knot sits on the surface of the fabric and should resemble a little bead.

LAZY DAISY STITCH

A version of Chain Stitch with separate loops held in place with a small stitch taken over the end. Take the needle under the fabric to the starting point for the next stitch. The stitches are often worked in a circle to make a simple flower design.

techniques

CROSS-STITCH

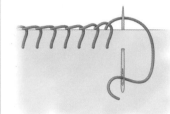

To work a row of cross stitch, make even, equally spaced diagonal stitches, working from bottom to top. Then go back across the row slanting the stitches in the opposite direction to complete the cross. Cross-stitch is very versatile because it can also be worked as a single stitch, in different sizes or elongated to change its shape.

BLANKET STITCH

This stitch is both decorative and functional and is often used in appliqué and for sealing the edges of fabric. Bring the needle through at the edge of the fabric. Push the needle back through the fabric a short distance from the edge and loop the thread under the needle. Pull the thread through to make the first stitch, then make another stitch to the right of this. Continue along the fabric.

RIBBON ROSE

1 Work five straight stitches in a circle as shown, using embroidery floss (thread). Change to narrow ribbon and bring it out near the center of the circle between two of the straight stitches.

2 Begin weaving the ribbon over and under the straight stitches, without catching the background fabric. Continue working around to complete the rose and then tie off the ribbon at the back.

LEVIATHAN STITCH

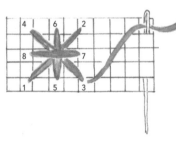

This stitch is a square shape double cross-stitch, made by working a single cross-stitch in the usual way and then working a second cross at right angles over the top of the first to make a simple eight-pointed star. Leviathan Stitch is usually worked as single stitches scattered across the design, rather than in rows or to make up a block of embroidery. The two cross-stitches can also be made in different color threads to create a different effect.

RIBBON FLOWER

Work this ribbon embroidery using fairly narrow ribbon on openweave fabric. Pull the ribbon through at the center of the flower position and then stitch back through the ribbon a short distance away to create a ribbon petal with a folded tip. Repeat the stitch in a circle to form a flower head shape. This same stitch can also be used individually to create leaves.

Knitting

The knitting projects in this book are very simple and only use the basic techniques.

MAKING A SLIP KNOT

For the first stitch on the needle, make a slip knot.

1 Wrap the yarn loosely around the first two fingers of your left hand, crossing the yarn over once. Place a needle under the back strand of the yarn and pull through to make a loop on the needle.

2 Gently slip your fingers away from the loop and lightly pull the end on the left to tighten the knot. It should be firm on the needle but not so tight that you can't fit the other needle through it.

HOLDING THE NEEDLES

The needle in your left hand is held lightly over the top. You can either hold the right-hand needle in the same way, or like a pen, so it rests in the crook of your thumb. Choose which feels most comfortable.

CASTING ON

1 Place the right needle into the slip knot from front to back. Wrap the yarn round the back of the tip of the right needle.

2 Pull the stitch through by bringing the tip of the right needle through to the front. Draw the loop out more by pulling it gently using the right-hand needle.

3 Make a stitch by catching the loop with the tip of the left-hand needle under the loop, so it moves onto the left-hand needle. Repeat until you have the required number of stitches.

BINDING (CASTING) OFF

With the yarn at the back, knit two stitches. Using the tip of the left-hand needle, lift the first stitch over the second stitch and off the needle. Knit the next stitch and continue as before until only one stitch remains. Cut or break the yarn, pull the tail end through the loop and pull gently to secure the last stitch.

techniques

KNIT STITCH

Knit stitches are worked with the yarn at the back.

1 Place the right-hand needle into the first stitch as shown. Supporting the needles in the crossed position, take the strand of yarn and wrap it round the back of the tip of the right-hand needle toward the front.

2 Pull the stitch through by bringing the tip of the right-hand needle through to the front.

3 Gently slide the loop off the left-hand needle by easing it off the tip with your left index (first) finger. Pull the stitch gently to secure in place on the right-hand needle.

PURL STITCH

Purl stitches are worked with the yarn at the front.

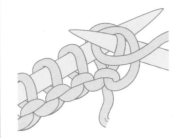

1 Push the right needle into the first stitch as shown. Supporting the needles in the crossed position, take the strand of yarn and wrap it round through the middle of the crossed needles and around the right-hand needle to the front.

2 Pull the stitch through by taking the tip of the right-hand needle through to the back.

3 Gently slide the loop off the left-hand needle by easing it off the tip with your left index (first) finger. Pull the stitch gently to secure in place on the right-hand needle.

KNIT 2 TOGETHER

Using the right-hand needle, knit two stitches together knitwise and then slip them both off the left-hand needle.

INCREASING

Put the right hand needle through the bar (horizontal strand from the previous row between two stitches) from front to back, slip the strand onto the left-hand needle, and then knit through the back of the strand. This makes one increased stitch.

STOCKINETTE (STOCKING) STITCH

This is created by working alternate knit and purl rows and can be worked over any number of stitches. All the smooth stitches will be on one side of the fabric and all the ridges will be on the other side. Usually the smooth side is used as the RS, or visible side of the fabric—but you can use the other side for a more textured look.

Crochet

All the crochet projects in this book are written using US pattern terminology. In this section we explain how to work the stitches and give both their US and UK names.

YARN OVER HOOK (YARN ROUND HOOK)

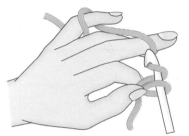

To create a stitch, catch the yarn from behind with the hook pointed upward. As you pull the yarn through the loop, turn the hook so it faces downward and slide the yarn through the loop. The loop on the hook should be loose so the hook slides through easily.

CHAIN

1 Wrap the yarn over the hook and pull it through the loop on the hook, creating a new loop on the hook. Continue in this way to create a chain of the required length or number of stitches.

2 Pull through, creating a new loop on the hook. Continue in this way to create a chain of the required length.

CHAIN RING/CIRCLE

This is also sometimes called a magic ring. Start by making the number of chains in the pattern.

1 Insert the hook into the first chain (not into the slip knot), yarn over hook, then pull the yarn through the chain and through the loop on the hook to make a circle.

2 You will now have a circle ready according to your pattern.

SLIP STITCH

A slip stitch doesn't create any height and is often used as the last stitch in a row to create a smooth and even round.

1 To make a slip stitch: put the hook through the work, yarn over (round) hook.

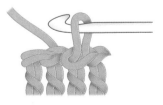

2 Pull the yarn through both the work and through the loop on the hook at the same time.

techniques

133

SINGLE CROCHET (US)
DOUBLE CROCHET (UK)

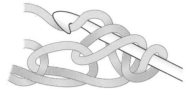

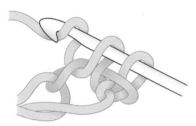

1 Insert the hook into your work, yarn over hook and pull the yarn through the work. You will then have two loops on the hook.

2 Yarn over hook again and pull through the two loops on the hook. You will then have one loop left on the hook.

STITCH VARIATIONS

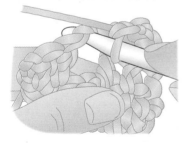

Crochet stitches are usually worked under both strands of the stitch, but in some patterns in this book you work into the gap between two stitches in the row below, so place the hook into the hole between two stitches and not into a stitch.

HALF DOUBLE (US)
HALF TREBLE (UK)

1 Before inserting the hook into the work, wrap the yarn over the hook and put the hook through the work with the yarn wrapped around.

2 Yarn over hook again and pull through the work (you will now have three loops on the hook).

3 Yarn over hook and pull the yarn through all three loops. You will be left with one loop on the hook. Note that whichever stitch you are working, when you have completed it you will always be left with one loop on the hook.

DOUBLE CROCHET (US)
TREBLE (UK)

1 Before inserting the hook into the work, wrap the yarn over the hook and put the hook through the work with the yarn already wrapped over.

2 Yarn over hook again and pull through the work (you now have three loops on the hook). Yarn over hook again, pull the yarn through the first two loops on the hook (you now have two loops on the hook).

3 Pull the yarn through the remaining two loops again. You will be left with one loop on the hook.

JOINING NEW YARN

This is usually done at the start of a new row/round. Insert the hook as normal into the stitch. Holding a short length of the new yarn behind the work, wrap it around the hook and pull a loop through. Continue to work the stitch following the instructions in the pattern and using the new yarn.

MAKING ROWS

When making straight rows you need to make a turning chain at the start of the row to create the height you need for the stitch you are working with, as follows:

Single crochet (US) = 1 chain
Half double (US) = 2 chain
Double crochet (US) = 3 chain

MAKING ROUNDS

When working in rounds the work is not turned so you are always working from one side. Depending on the pattern you are working, a "round" can be square. Again, you will need to make a turning chain to create the height you need for the stitch you are working, as listed under Making Rows (above).

To keep count of where you are in the pattern, you can place a stitch marker at the beginning of each round; a piece of yarn in a contrasting color is useful for this. Loop the stitch marker into the first stitch; when you have made a round and reached the point where the stitch marker is, work this stitch, take out the stitch marker from the previous round and put it back into the first stitch of the new round.

SINGLE CROCHET 2 STITCHES TOGETHER (US)
DOUBLE CROCHET 2 STITCHES TOGETHER (UK)

This stitch is used to decrease when shaping and the basic technique is the same whichever stitch you are working.

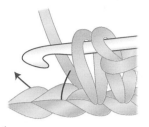

1 Insert the hook into your work, yarn over the hook and pull the yarn through the work. You will then have two loops on the hook.

2 Yarn over the hook again and pull through all three loops on the hook. You will then have one loop on the hook.

INCREASING

To increase the number of stitches, work several stitches into one stitch in the row below. The artwork shows three double crochet (US) being worked, but the basic technique is the same for all stitches. Working groups of stitches like this, but skipping the same number of stitches between the groups, will not increase the overall number of stitches but will create a simple open crochet design.

POPCORN OR BOBBLE

This stitch is used in the Crochet Coaster and in the Seaside Crochet Blanket. The artwork shows four double crochet (US) stitches being joined to make a popcorn or bobble, but the basic technique is the same no matter which stitch you work or how many stitches you join. Slip the hook out of the top of the last stitch worked, insert it into the top of the first stitch and then back into the last stitch. Pull the last stitch through the first stitch.

FASTENING OFF

Cut the yarn leaving a tail of approx 4 in.(10 cm). Pull the tail all the way through the last loop.

techniques

C

D

Yarn and felt
flower wreath p33
E

A

B

F

Clay heart
bunting p40

Honeycomb
patchwork
pillow
p10

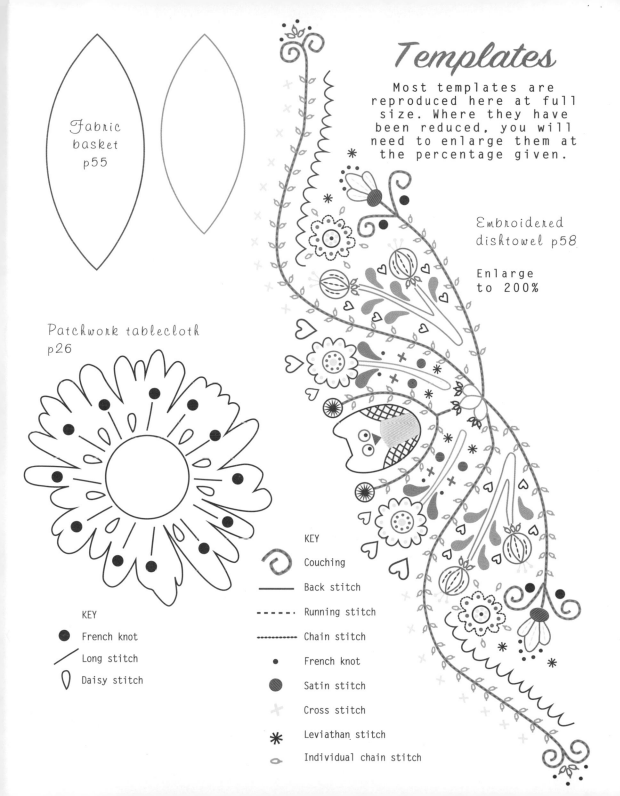

Templates

Most templates are reproduced here at full size. Where they have been reduced, you will need to enlarge them at the percentage given.

Fabric basket p55

Embroidered dishtowel p58

Enlarge to 200%

Patchwork tablecloth p26

KEY
- ● French knot
- ╱ Long stitch
- ◊ Daisy stitch

KEY
- ↻ Couching
- ⎯ Back stitch
- ----- Running stitch
- ·········· Chain stitch
- · French knot
- ● Satin stitch
- ✕ Cross stitch
- ✳ Leviathan stitch
- ⬯ Individual chain stitch

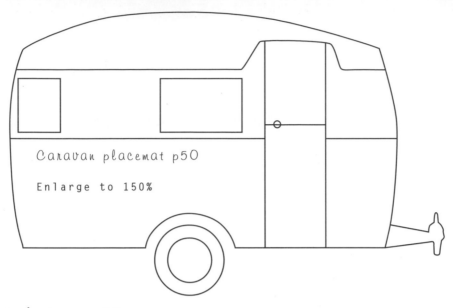

Caravan placemat p50

Enlarge to 150%

Cross-stitch picture p76

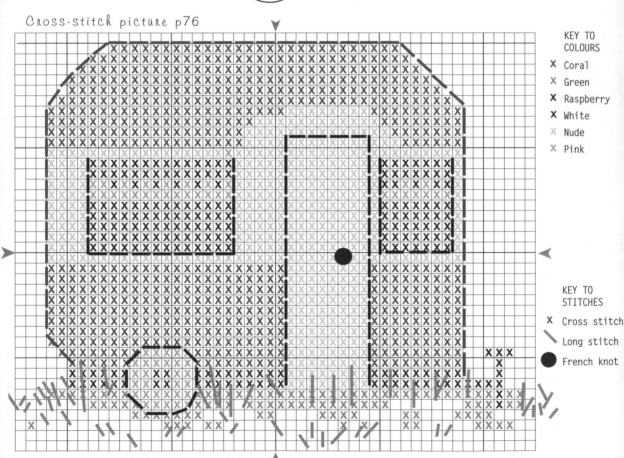

KEY TO
COLOURS

X Coral
X Green
X Raspberry
X White
X Nude
X Pink

KEY TO
STITCHES

X Cross stitch
/ Long stitch
● French knot

12369

Upcycled
vintage plates
p92

Enlarge
to 200%

Dreamcatcher
p90

Embroidered towel
p109

Enlarge to
200%

Pocket tidy p106
Enlarge to 200%

Funky flowers
shower cap
p104

Striped knitted tea cozy p44
and Pompom garland p97
Cut 2

Windbreak
p122

Enlarge
to 200%

Suppliers

NORTH AMERICA

A.C. Moore
888-226-6673
Stores nationwide
www.acmoore.com

Amy Butler Design
218 mt Parnassus Drive,
Ganville, OH 43023
740-587-2841
www.amybutlerdesign.com

Britex Fabrics
146 Geary Street
San Francisco, CA 94108
415-392-2910
www.britexfabrics.com

Buy Fabrics
8967 Rand Ave
Daphne, Al 36526
877-625-2889
www.buyfabrics.com

Cia's Palette
4155 Grand Ave S
Minneapolis, MN 55409
612-229-5227
www.ciaspalette.com

Discount Fabrics USA
108 N. Carroll St.
Thurmont, MD 21788
301-271-2266
www.discountfabricsusacorp.com

Fabricville
855-533-2675
Stores nationwide
www.fabricville.com

J & O Fabrics
8101 Frankford Ave,
Philadelphia, PA 19136
856-663-2121
www.jandofabrics.com

Hobby Lobby
Stores nationwide
www.hobbylobby.com

Jo-Ann Fabric and Craft Store
1-888-739-4120
Stores nationwide
www.joann.com

Michaels
1-800-642-4235
Stores nationwide
www.michaels.com

Purl Soho
147 Sullivan Street
New York, NY 10012
800-597-7875
www.purlsoho.com

Rowan Yarns
Online store locator
www.knitrowan.com

Tinsel Trading Company
1659 San Pablo Ave,
Berkeley, CA 94702
510-370-2149
www.tinseltrading.com

UK

**Abakhan Fabrics,
Hobby and Home**
www.abakhan.co.uk

Borovick's
16 Berwick Street
London W1F 0HP
020 7437 2180
www.borovickfabricsltd.co.uk

The Cloth House
47 Berwick Street
London W1F 8SJ
020 7437 5155
www.clothhouse.com

Fabric Galore
52–54 Lavender Hill
Battersea
London SW11 5RH
020 7738 9589
www.fabricsgalore.co.uk

Hobby Craft
Stores nationwide
www.hobbycraft.co.uk

John Lewis
Stores nationwide
www.johnlewis.com

Kleins
5 Noel Street
London W1F 8GD
020 7437 6162
www.kleins.co.uk

Liberty
Regent Street
London W1B 5AH
020 7734 1234
www.libertylondon.co.uk

VV Rouleaux
102 Marylebone Lane
London W1U 2QD
020 7224 5179
www.vvrouleaux.com

Rowan Yarns
Stores nationwide
www.knitrowan.com

Index

ACKNOWLEDGMENTS

We would like to thank the team at CICO for ensuring that every element of the book looks great. It has been a pleasure to work with you.

We would also like to say a big thank you to each other! We met ten years ago at the University in Huddersfield, where we were both studying for a degree in Textile Crafts; we soon became great friends and have been mulling this book idea over ever since. We're so pleased that it has finally come to fruition, despite the fact that we now live and work at opposite ends of the country.

Thanks to the men in our lives, Danny and Jamie, who have to live with our piles of fabric, yarn, and trims, and do so without too much complaint!

This brings us to our final thanks—or rather dedication. Whilst writing this book Charlotte gave birth to a lovely baby boy named Syd. She certainly won't be able to flick through this book without remembering the day she went into labor! So, on that note, we would like to dedicate this book to baby Sydney Dawson George born on Sunday, August 5, 2012. Here's to many happy years of crafting fun!

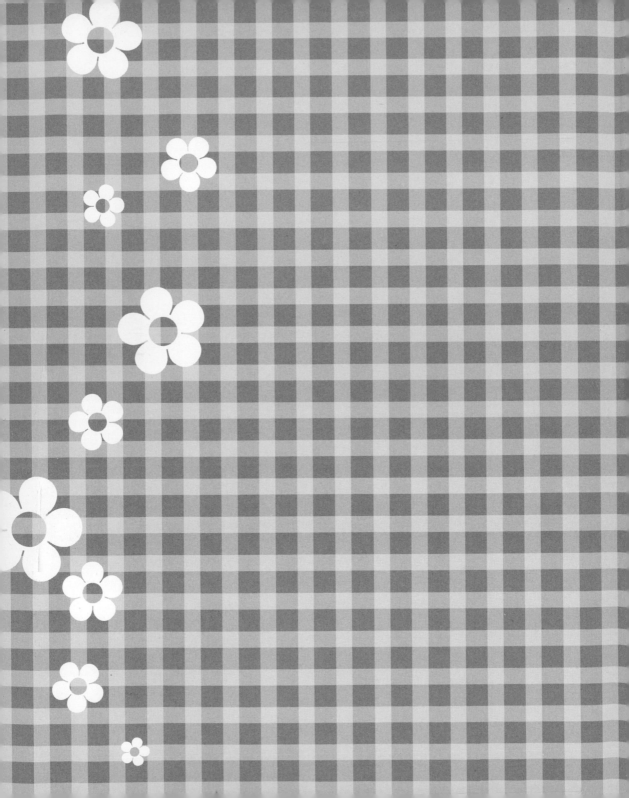